MW01089447

"I read this book with tears rolling down my cheeks yet with joy in my heart. Richard tells his story of young love, decades of faithfulness and finally of retching grief in a personal and poignant manner. This book is for those who are grieving ... as well as for those who dread what grief might feel like. I am determined, after reading *"Letters for Brenda"*, to love more fully and to embrace the joy that belongs solely to today."

"Thank you, dear Richard. Thank you for sharing your journey of grief with all of us. As I pondered your words birthed in the valley of the shadow of death, a determination arose in me. I am determined to love well and to live well. I am determined to trust God with tomorrow and to dig deeply for joy in the treasure of today. Thank you for teaching us that God is faithful in all seasons of life."

CAROL MCLEOD | A girl who loves Jesus
Bible Teacher and Author | Podcaster and Blogger

The transparency of soul and marriage life revealed by my brother Richard is one of his great traits as a man, a minister, and an author. The truths in *Letters for Brenda* have caused me to "slam on the brakes" to reassess aspects of my life and my busyness as my wife and I continue to be blessed by our 50 plus years of marriage. *Letters for Brenda* will not only encourage, strengthen, and bless those who are in a valley of grief but will also help married couples value their commitment to their spouse and will give insight into how to transform normal moments into magical moments.

DONALD EXLEY | Missionary and Church Planter

I've just finished reading *"Letters for Brenda."* While deeply personal it addresses a universal experience—grief following the death of a spouse. It provides hope and peace in the seemingly endless journey through the valley of the shadow of death. Truly weeping may last through the night but joy comes in the morning. Anointed and timely words!

LINDA CARGILL | Author,
"Survival 101 Practical advice for Ministers Wives"

During my years of pastoral ministry, I would always give a copy of Richard Exley's book *"When You Lose Someone You Love"* to a grieving spouse when their husband or wife died. It was always helpful counsel for those who needed to be comforted. After the loss of his wife, Brenda, due to cancer, Richard has now experienced the depths of grief in a way that he did not really know when he wrote the previous book on grief. This new book, *"Letters for Brenda"* is a powerful compilation of personal letters Richard penned to Brenda to help him process his deep grief. It is real, it is raw, it is powerful. At times it is filled with despair as Richard battles his "aloneness," but at the same time it is filled with faith. Another must-read from Richard Exley.

THE REVEREND BOB COOK | National Director
Senior Adult Ministry for the Assemblies of God

"Letters to Brenda" expresses a bittersweet mixture of the depth of loss, raw emotion and painful grief. Richard Exley, in a way only he can, mingles his extraordinary grief at losing his beloved wife, Brenda, with words of comfort, peace, sweetness, and hope. The letters will draw your heart into the pain of another while simultaneously bestowing a new perspective of gratitude for the life you've been given. Richard teaches us all how to grieve well and how to find a deeper walk with Jesus in the process.

MARIYNDA LYNCH

"Letters for Brenda" by Richard Exley is a poignant and heartrending autobiographical journey through the depths of grief following the loss of his beloved wife in 2022. Having known Brenda personally, I can attest that this book beautifully captures the essence of their profound love story through heartfelt letters. Each account is a testament to the enduring bond they shared, bringing tears to my eyes and solace to my heart. Richard's ability to articulate the complex emotions of loss is truly remarkable, and his words resonate deeply with anyone who has experienced a similar journey. As he eloquently puts it, "If I have written these well, you will get in touch with your feelings while reading about mine." In endorsing this book, I echo the

sentiment that Richard has indeed done exceptionally well in sharing a love story that transcends time and speaks to the universal experience of grief.

> BARBRA RUSSELL, MA, LPC,
> Author of *"Yes! I Said No! How to Set Healthy Boundaries and Increase Your Self Esteem."*

"Letters to Brenda is filled with vulnerability and raw emotion and I was moved to tears as I read these beautiful letters. Grief is such a lonely journey, but Richard Exley invites the reader into his soul as he walks through his own grief and in doing so brings real hope and a glimmer of light to the reader. I was deeply moved as I read these heartwarming letters and encourage anyone who has lost a loved one to read, *"Letters to Brenda."*

> CAROL HOLDERNESS

In *"Letters for Brenda"* Richard Exley dares to do what few others will do. He candidly shares the myriad of emotions he experienced in the empty days and exhausting months of loneliness following the death of his wife. The intensity of his grief only serves to make the joy that comes in the "mourning" more wonderful. As he testifies, our good God, who never leaves and never forsakes, transformed the ashes of his grief into the beauty of new beginnings.

> RUTH MERRELL | Missionary
> Co-founder of the Oral Learners Initiative

"Letters for Brenda" was never intended to be published. In the beginning these letters were simply the outpouring of Richard's heart broken by unimaginable grief. As such they are intensely personal reflections on a journey of fifty-six years of love, life, and ministry. Now Richard shares these intimate moments with us all. And invites us to share the joy that surprised him in the midst of his mourning.

> JOHN MERRELL | Missionary
> Founder of the Oral Learners Initiative and former Director of International Media Ministries

In *"Letters for Brenda,"* Richard Exley shares his personal journey through grief. Reading these letters is like someone giving voice to what our grieving hearts have experienced and yet are often unable to express. It is raw and transparent but leads to a place of comfort and ultimately healing for all who will allow the work of the Holy Spirit to bring healing to their place of loss. I highly recommend *"Letters for Brenda"* for anyone who has lost someone dear to their heart. Reading it is truly a "journey from grief to gratefulness."

KAREN HARDIN
President, PriorityPR Group & Literary Agency
President, City-by-City Prayer Network & Awake Oklahoma

Grief is universal to all cultures but how one personally overcomes the death of a loved one can be uniquely personal. In *"Letters to Brenda,"* Richard uses his writing to lighten his "... walk through the valley of the shadow of death." He does so in a way that allows the reader to experience both compassion and hope.

ROBERT J. EXLEY, PhD | President of Alvin Community College

Anyone who has suffered loss knows that you can be utterly alone even in a crowd. Through Richard Exley's *"Letters For Brenda"*, that deep seated sorrow and aloneness finds a friend. Someone who understands what you are experiencing. It, in turn, helps you begin to process your pain and in the processing, you can begin to remember the joy. This is a must read for those walking through a season of great grief.

LEAH STARR BAKER | Author of "The Bunko Babes"

There are very few people I know who have the courage to share their grief for all the world to experience with them. My friend, Richard Exley is a rare breed who is willing to lay bare his broken heart and grieving soul openly and in such a manner that others may also find peace, comfort, and healing. Passionate, heartfelt, and desperately sincere...*Letters For Brenda* is a very special gift. To my brother in Christ, Richard, Thank you for who you are and your willingness to minister to me and others, as God brings peace and healing to you.

DR. CHUCK STECKER
Executive Director | A Chosen Generation

Tears were running down my cheeks as I read Richard's text telling me that Brenda was nearing death, Instantly I had a flashback to 1978. My 2-year-old daughter was playing with her little Barbie and Ken dolls except she was calling them Brenda and Richard. How appropriate, I thought, for Brenda and Richard were the perfect couple. I couldn't help thinking, how can there be a Richard without a Brenda? I couldn't help wondering how Richard would make it without her. In *Letters to Brenda*, he tells us how he made it. He openly shares his heartbreak and all that it encompassed—emotionally, physically and spiritually. Best of all He affirms that Jesus is enough to carry our grief, heal our hearts and stop the attack of the enemy in our darkest hour. Walk with him as he openly shares his walk through grief into healing.

ELAINE WELLS

As scripture declares, "Weeping may endure for the night but joy comes in the morning." Carol and I have witnessed and journeyed with Richard through one of the most difficult chapters of his life. Richard and Brenda were a team in life and ministry and touched so many lives in their journey. Their love story included each other and many others. We watched Richard serve Brenda in her last year of life with such love and affection and witnessed him try to fulfill all her wishes. It was both heart touching and heart wrenching. We were able to see the transitions first hand that he is sharing in this book. His journey from extreme mourning to the point of celebrating the life they shared together was not an easy road. I believe this book will give others hope in the midst of the direst circumstances they may face in life.

KEITH AND CAROL BUTLER
Pastors Church on the Hill | Berryville, Arkansas

Have you lost a spouse, a parent, or a child? Has grief overtaken your joy? Have you said to yourself, "This is more than I can bear?" In *Letters for Brenda* Richard Exley offers words of hope and healing. These letters helped Richard work through his grief and loneliness. While the terrible feeling of loss has not totally departed, with God's help he has learned to be grateful for their time together. As you walk with him on his journey from grief to gratefulness may the Lord do the same for you.

THOMAS HARRISON, PhD | Tulsa, Oklahoma
Author, Minister, and Speaker
Move Up! Don't Give Up!
Factual Accounts of Courage, Hope, and Inspiration

"Let me tell you a bit about Richard Exley. First off, he has had a profound influence on my personal and writing life. God brought him into my journey at the most critical time and he spoke words of life-direction and transformation. I call him my "Pastor of Writing." As an author, Richard's books have equally impacted me, both fiction and non-fiction. I have a section in my library just for his books. What makes me excited about *Letters for Brenda* is I watched him love her for years as they exemplified what a godly and romantic marriage should be. I also watched as Richard poured himself into caring for Brenda during her illness. He laid aside his beloved writing, speaking, and pastoring as his calling became full-time caretaker to the love of his life. I was inspired by him. That same emotion and love that he poured into Brenda are poured into the writing of *Letters for Brenda*. You will be moved to tears and to love deeper."

MAX DAVIS
Author and New York Times Bestselling collaborator

Letters To Brenda is a deeply heartfelt story of one man's journey through grief. What makes it unique is the fact that it often expresses what we feel in our heart in times of grief but are unable to put it into words. Even though it chronicles Richard's journey though grief, it reminds us of the hope and comfort that is in ours in Christ and how God does provide for new beginnings. I plan to get several copies for friends who are dealing with the death of a spouse. As you read it, may the Lord use Richard's words to help you in your own journey of losing a loved one.

REV. MIKE BUIE | Pastor

LETTERS FOR BRENDA

A JOURNEY FROM GRIEF TO GRATEFULNESS

RICHARD EXLEY

WORD & SPIRIT
PUBLISHING

Letters for Brenda: A Journey from Grief to Gratefulness
Copyright © 2023 by Richard Exley
ISBN: 978-1-685730-31-4

Published by Word and Spirit Publishing
P.O. Box 701403
Tulsa, Oklahoma 74170
wordandspiritpublishing.com

CONTENTS

It was easy to dance when our lives were filled with music and laughter, but when death took you from me, the lights went out, and the music died. Still, I am determined to keep dancing—I know that's what you would want me to do. But if I am going to dance in the dark, I will have to cling more tightly to Jesus, follow His lead more closely, especially when I can't hear the music. If I can do that, I believe I will discover a strength that will sustain me through these dark times.

Now I whisper a prayer into the darkness: "Dance with me, Lord Jesus. Hold me close and restore my joy."

PREFACE

Let me say right up front that *Letters for Brenda* is unashamedly autobiographical. It is my story—a chronological account of how grief manifested itself in my life following my wife's death and how I dealt with it. We had been married for fifty-six years when she left this world, and following her death, my emotions were all over the place. My faith remained strong, but my heart was breaking. A few days after her passing, the responsibilities of day-to-day life required that my family and friends return to their homes, leaving me to fare for myself. Never had I felt so alone. Not lonely. Alone. In order to process my grief, I needed to talk about it, but I had no one to talk to. Besides, some of the things I needed to talk about were so personal, so intimate, I couldn't imagine sharing them with just anyone. Who would understand? Only Brenda, my soul mate—but she was gone, and she wasn't coming back.

Out of desperation, I decided that if I couldn't talk to her, I would write her a series of letters. From time to time, I read a letter, or a portion of a letter, to a close friend. At other times, I posted an excerpt on my Facebook page. The responses were overwhelmingly positive. Grieving people, especially those who had lost a spouse, thanked me for expressing what they felt but had never been able to put into words. Friends and family members said that for the first time, they truly understood what a grieving spouse experienced. Not a few suggested I turn my letters into a book, thus this small volume.

I will always love Brenda, and she will live forever in my heart. Because I have done my grief work, I am free to remember the rich life we shared, rather than just the trauma of her death. These letters are my way of saying goodbye to her. Although they are deeply personal, I share them with you in hopes that they will help you process your own grief. If I have written them well, you will get in touch with your feelings while reading about mine. Hopefully you will laugh and cry over a lifetime of memories and in the process find healing and comfort. Writing them was therapeutic for me, and I trust that reading them will be healing for you.

Richard Exley
August 30, 2023
Fort Worth, Texas

THE FIRST LETTER

I want you to know what happens to a Christian when he dies so that when it happens, you will not be full of sorrow, as those are who have no hope.

1 THESSALONIANS 4:13 TLB

Dearest Brenda:

The unspeakable has happened. Cancer has done its evil work, and death has stolen you from me. When I stepped out onto the patio adjoining your room at the Circle of Life hospice facility to give Leah (our daughter) a call to update her, you were chatting with friends from Shreveport. Hardly had Leah answered the phone before Susan rushed out to tell me the nurse said it looked like you were leaving us. I handed her my cell phone and hurried to your bedside. You were unconscious and struggling to breathe. Taking your limp hand in mine, I began to pray, not for God to heal you, but for Him to make your passage from this life to the next as painless and as peaceful as possible.

As I held your hand next to my cheek, I began praying Scriptures and quoting the great hymns of the faith. I wanted you to leave this world without fear, with the promises of God's Word filling your heart and your mind. I hope you could hear me and that you were comforted. I continued to pray passionately for the better part of an hour, reciting all the Scriptures I knew and quoting every hymn I could remember. Finally, exhaustion overcame me, and for the next ten or eleven hours, I sat beside you, numb with grief. As the first hint of daylight was breaching the darkness, you took one final breath and then slipped into eternity, into the presence of your Lord and Savior, whom you loved so passionately and served so faithfully.

Our dear friends Tommy and Shirley King had remained with me the entire night, and at that moment Shirley said, "I think she's gone."

"Are you sure?" I asked, still not able to comprehend that you, the love of my life, were really gone.

I continued to hold your lifeless hand as Shirley slipped out to call the hospice nurse. I kept thinking, *How can this be?* When the ambulance had brought you to the hospice facility on Sunday afternoon to have your abdomen drained, we thought we would be returning home on Monday evening, Tuesday morning at the latest. Although we had asked the Lord to take you home quickly if He wasn't going to heal you supernaturally, I didn't expect it to be so soon. But He had answered our prayers, and now it was breaking my heart. *How am I going to live without you?* my heart cried. *You have been a part of my life since we were just kids.*

After my father died, my mother was grief-stricken. Sitting with me on our porch overlooking Beaver Lake, she told me, "I can't do this, Richard. I can't go on living without your father." In an instant, my mind returned to the death of my baby sister, when she was just a few weeks old. Taking mother's hand in mine, I asked, "How did you do it when Carolyn died?"

Choking back her tears, she said, "When Carolyn died, I had your father. When I cried, he held me. When I needed to talk, he listened to me. Now I have no one."

On that sunlit afternoon, her words made no sense to me. What did she mean, she had no one? She had her four children and their spouses. She had nine grandchildren and a host of friends. Now I understand. Although a loving family and a host of caring friends surround me, I, too, feel like I have no one. Now that you are gone, I feel totally alone.

With whom can I share my heart? Who will listen to what I've written? Who will take communion with me? Whose hand will I hold as I drift toward sleep in the darkness of the night? Who, I ask you—who?

That's why I have chosen to write these letters. If I can't talk to you, then I will write to you, pouring out all the pain and sorrow, all the grief and loneliness that threatens to overwhelm me. Tears have become a part of every day, and I am weeping as I write this. Still, as hard as this is, I wouldn't bring you back even if I could. When you decided not to take any more treatments, I told you, "It's okay, baby. Who would want to stay here when they could go to heaven?"

Having said that, I must add that I would give almost anything to spend one more day with you. I would give almost anything to take one more drive through Eureka Springs and to share one more evening on the porch overlooking Beaver Lake as the setting sun ushers in the "golden hour." I would give almost anything to go skinny-dipping with you one more time as the moon comes up over the lake or to sit with you by the fire as the season's first snow comes drifting down. I would give almost anything to take communion with you one more time and to hear you pray again. I would give almost anything to take your hand and whisper, "I love you," one more time as we drift toward sleep, wrapped in our love. To paraphrase Kris Kristofferson, I would trade all my tomorrows for a single yesterday holding you close.

There's so much more I could say, but I think I will save it for another letter.

With all my love forever,

P.S. Before I sign off, I must tell you that, as hard as this is—and it's the hardest thing I've ever had to do—at times Jesus has been more real to me than ever before. His near presence gives me comfort even when grief makes it impossible for me to pray. All I can do is say, "Jesus, Jesus," again and again, or pray in the Spirit, as silent tears stain my cheeks. His closeness does not take my grief away, but it does give me the strength to bear it.

THE SECOND LETTER

She speaks with wisdom,
and faithful instruction is on her tongue.

PROVERBS 31:26 NIV

Dearest Brenda:

Other than satellite TV, you had little or no use for technology. You refused to learn how to use a computer, you hated email and texting, Facebook was anathema, and you used your cell phone only as a last resort. You loved receiving cards, but you hated writing them. You would labor over a half-page note for the better part of a day, and a handwritten note from you was rare, a thing to be treasured. I often joked that if it weren't for me, we wouldn't have any friends.

I was the one who stayed in touch with them. I emailed them, texted, posted on Facebook, and talked via cell phone regularly. You often told your sister that you didn't have any friends, that all your friends were really my friends. I knew that wasn't true, but I couldn't convince you.

If you ever wondered about the love and loyalty of your friends, all doubts should have been removed when you entered the Circle of Life hospice facility in Bentonville, Arkansas. As word spread, friends began arriving from around the country. Lee and Barbara Clark drove in from Texas. Lee was the best man in our wedding, and Barbara was your best friend from high school. Although we had only connected rarely, as ministry took us to distant places, they dropped everything and rushed to your side. Frank Cargill, the former Oklahoma district superintendent, and his wife, Linda, came from Oklahoma City. Our pastor and his wife (Keith and Carol Butler) came from Berryville, Arkansas. Tommy and Shirley King drove in from Shreveport, Louisiana. They moved into a nearby extended-stay hotel and remained with us until you passed, leaving your bedside only to catch a few hours' sleep. Susan Cherry, your dear friend from Gateway Church, and her husband, Grant, also came, as did Charles and Vergie Walker. Soon your room was filled with your friends who loved you. Yes, **your** friends! They were my friends also, but they were truly your friends.

Maybe you didn't text or post on Facebook, but you knew how to make people feel special. You were good at that—maybe the best ever. In the eulogy she gave at your service, Ruth Merrell, your dearest friend, said, "Shortly after Richard and Brenda went to Gateway Church in Shreveport, John and I visited them. The women were having a ladies' fellowship, so Brenda and I went to the home where they were gathered. As usual, when Brenda walked in, everyone knew the prettiest girl in the room had arrived. Instead of her presence sucking the air out of the room, like most divas, Brenda brought her 'gracious magic.' She made her way around the room speaking to each lady, noticing something special about every woman present. Instead of feeling less, everyone felt 'more'—more loved, more accepted, and more beautiful than when they came."

And Ruth was right. You had a gift for making everyone feel special!

I was thinking about that as your friends filled your room at the hospice facility. There were a lot of hugs and tears, but some laughter, too. Susan had us all laughing as she recounted the first time you all met. As you may recall, the official board had invited me to interview with them for the senior pastor position at Gateway Church in Shreveport. While I was meeting with the board, their wives invited you to a "get acquainted" dinner. When it came time for you to share something about yourself, you simply said, "I'm pretty sure I am not the kind of pastor's wife you are looking for. I have no musical ability. I don't play the piano or sing. I don't lead worship or direct the choir. I don't teach a Bible class or lead the women's ministry."

As soon as the dinner was over, Susan called her husband and said, "I don't care what you have to do to get this guy to be our pastor, but whatever it is, do it. Sell the farm if you have to! His wife is a jewel. She's a keeper!"

I couldn't agree more. You are a keeper!

Only I didn't get to keep you. You weren't really mine, even though the Bible says a godly wife is a gift from the Lord. You were simply a gift *on loan from* God. For fifty-six years, He entrusted you to me. You were my dearest friend, my confidant, my partner in ministry, my lover, and my soul mate. Far too soon death took you away. Two previous times, you went to the doorway of death only to return: the first time when you had a massive hemorrhage following Leah's birth, and four years ago, when you had brain surgery to clip an aneurysm. This time it was uterine cancer, and this time you didn't return.

I should have realized how sick you were, but I think I was in denial. Although your abdomen filled with fluid, making it hard for you to breathe and impossible for you to eat more than a few bites, I still didn't get it. And you never complained, not once. Five weeks before you died, you were swimming in the lake with your nieces and their children. Who does that? And just three weeks before you passed, you were playing table games with Don and Melba and their grandchildren.

I thought I was prepared for your death, but now I know there is no way to prepare for something like this. We planned your funeral together—you chose the songs you wanted to be sung and the singers; you wanted Ruth to give the eulogy and my brother Don to preach the funeral message. You were so brave. I blinked back tears and struggled to hold myself together, but you were so matter-of-fact, as if planning your funeral was no big deal. You faced death the way you lived life: unafraid. Or, if you were afraid, you never let fear control you.

The only time I sensed fear, or maybe it was just uncertainty, was when you asked me how you would ever find me in heaven among those billions of people. Quick as a flash, I said, "I don't have any real scriptural basis for this, but since there is no time or distance in heaven, I believe that when you think, *I want to be with Richard*, I will instantly be right beside you." You smiled, and we never discussed it again. Thinking about it now, it gives me great joy to know that you want to be with me for eternity.

I spend a lot of time looking at the thousands of photos we took over the years. It is easier to remember the past than to imagine the future without you. Each photo evokes a memory, and I relive the moments that became our life. It is bittersweet, and I find myself whispering your name again and again as I blink back tears and try to swallow past the grief that has lodged in my throat. I wish I had loved you better, but I comfort myself with the knowledge that I loved you with all of me, as much as I was capable of loving anyone. Maybe I could have loved you better, but I could not have loved you more.

As I grieve, staring into the darkness on these long winter nights, I encourage myself with the knowledge that you are not really dead, just gone. In fact, you are more alive than you have ever been, for Jesus said, "I am the resurrection, and the life: he that believeth in me, though he were dead, yet shall he live" (John 11:25 KJV). One day I will join you, and we will spend eternity together in that place where there is no more sickness or death.

That doesn't take my pain away, but it does give me the strength to bear it.

With all my love forever,

[signature: Richard]

THE THIRD LETTER

Honor her for all that her hands have done,
and let her works bring her praise at the city gate.

PROVERBS 31:31 NIV

Dearest Brenda:

Your passing has left a huge hole in my heart, and each day is simply an endless journey through the valley of the shadow of death. It seems all the light has gone out of my life, and I am wandering in the dark, but I am not alone. Jesus is with me! When friends ask how I am doing, I tell them that my heart is broken and my emotions are all over the place, but that my faith is strong.

As I think back over the fifty-six years we were married, the things that stand out are not the special events—except for the birth of our daughter. They were not a trip to Hawaii, nor our daughter's wedding, nor the births of our grandchildren, not even our fiftieth anniversary. Rather, it is the ordinary things I remember. Little things, which at first glance hardly seemed worth mentioning. Yet as the years went by, they become daily rituals nourishing the soul of our marriage. And it's those mundane details that molded the character of our relationship.

I mean, whoever speaks of the simple pleasure of coming home to familiar sounds—the hum of the vacuum cleaner, bathwater running, conversation from the other room—yet these were the sounds of our marriage. And the smells—skin cream and shampoo, clothes fresh from the dryer, furniture polish and coffee brewing. Ordinary things easily taken for granted, hardly noticed, until they are gone.

When you died, all of that changed. Now sounds are just sounds, and smells are just smells, nothing holy or sacred about them. Bathwater running is just that, nothing more, and furniture polish smells sterile, antiseptic, not like love at all. No one whispers my name into the bedtime darkness, and when I unconsciously fling my arm across the other side of the bed in the wee hours of the morning, there is no sleeping form, no comforting presence. I was once a beloved husband; now I'm a grieving man.

As I browse through the hundreds of photos chronicling our life and ministry, I remind myself that we were blessed. You were my best friend, my partner in ministry and the love of my life. Nothing, not even death, can take that away. How fortunate I was; how fortunate I am. I have a choice. I can rage at the unfairness of life, or I can praise the Lord. I choose to praise Him—and make no mistake, it is a daily choice, sometimes a minute-by-minute choice.

Even in this dark place, even in this valley of the shadow of death, there are glimmers of light. For instance, just a few days before you went to the Circle of Life hospice facility, Deuce (our only grandson) had a life-changing encounter with the Lord. He was called into the ministry, and he enrolled in Valley Forge Christian University to prepare for the mission field. You had prayed for him for years, and when he shared the news, you replied, "Now I can die in peace."

A glimmer of light in this dark place.

When Leah learned your time was short, she and Deuce flew in from upstate New York. The ten days they spent with us were especially blessed. Knowing how much you loved Christmas, Leah and Alexia (our granddaughter) put up your Christmas tree. For two days, you sat in the recliner in the living room watching them decorate while listening to Christmas music and reminiscing about Christmases past. When you told me you hoped you could make it to

Christmas, I had to leave the room. My heart was breaking. I knew that wasn't going to happen—and it didn't. Six days later, you left this world for a better place.

By Saturday evening, the eighth day of their visit, you were physically and emotionally exhausted. Although it had only been five days since the doctors had drained the fluid from your abdomen, it was swollen again, making it difficult for you to breathe and impossible for you to eat more than two or three small bites. Leaving Leah, Deuce, and Alexia at the table in the kitchen, I helped you to the bedroom. Once I got you settled in bed, I lay down beside you and took your hand in mine. The television was on, but the volume was muted, and we could hear laughter and the murmur of voices from the kitchen.

We hadn't heard anything like that in nearly five years. In 2017, Alexia and her parents had a falling-out, and she had come to live with us. They still loved each other, but the wounds they had inflicted on each other were painfully raw, and communication was strained. Now they were laughing and talking, reminiscing about childhood memories as if they had never been estranged. Undoubtedly the looming presence of your death made them realize how precious family relationships are. Turning to me, you said, "If it took cancer and my impending death to restore their relationships, it was worth it."

I squeezed your hand, but I didn't say anything. I couldn't. Later, as I lay in the dark staring at the ceiling as you struggled to breathe, I couldn't help thinking that your willingness to sacrifice yourself for your family personified who you were. Cancer wasn't your choice, and you would have chosen life if you could have, but you didn't have a choice. Still, if cancer and a premature death was what it took to heal your family, I know you would do it again.

More glimmers of light in this dark place.

As I close this letter, I remind myself that even in this tragedy, I have reasons to be thankful. I'm thankful we did not realize you would never be coming home to Emerald Pointe when we drove to the hospice facility that Sunday afternoon. Because you expected to return home in a couple of days, you were spared the trauma of telling Bailey (your dog) goodbye, and you were spared the grief of knowing you were leaving your beautiful home for the last time. I'm thankful the Lord answered our prayers and took you home quickly and with a minimum of suffering. The hospice nurses told me they had never witnessed a more peaceful death. And I'm thankful the Lord allowed you to die before I did so you never have to bear the grief I am living with.

More glimmers of light in this dark place.

It will be a long time before I stop grieving, if I ever do, but I am determined to season my grief with gratefulness. In time, the pain of your death should diminish to be replaced by the memories of the rich life we shared. Until that happens, the presence of the Lord and the hope of eternal life give me the strength to live each day.

With all my love forever,

Richard

THE FOURTH LETTER

The LORD is close to the brokenhearted;
he rescues those whose spirits are crushed.

PSALMS 34:18 NLT

Dearest Brenda:

It has now been nearly four months since you left me for a better place. How I wish we had gone together. Life without you isn't really life at all. I find myself wandering through the house whispering your name. It makes no sense. I know you are not here, but still I do it. And when I awaken in the night to use the bathroom, I slip out of bed as quietly as I can to keep from disturbing you. Dumb, isn't it? But old habits are hard to break.

This is your favorite time of the year—Thanksgiving and Christmas. Just last year, you decorated the front porch with fall colors for Thanksgiving and then decorated it again with wreaths, garlands, and colored lights for Christmas. It was snowing when you finished, and we huddled together on the porch hoping for a white Christmas. Well, Thanksgiving has come and gone, and Christmas is now just days away, and the porch is bare, desolate really, like my life. Someone suggested that maybe I should decorate it. I just smiled and never gave their suggestion a second thought. Sure, I miss the decorations and the artistic flare you gave to everything you did, but it's not just the decorations I miss. It's you!

I spoke at the senior Christmas dinner at Life Church in Midlothian a few days ago, and the next night I spoke at the sectional ministers and wives Christmas dinner in Fort Worth. The decorations were attractive, the meal was sumptuous, and the entertainment was fun. You would have loved it. The thing that stood out for me was not the camaraderie or the fun and games, but the empty chair. At both dinners, we were seated at round tables for six or eight. At the table where I was seated, there were three couples, myself, and an empty chair. Why someone didn't think to remove that stupid chair is beyond me. I'm not upset. Well, maybe a little, but before losing you, I probably would not have thought of it, either. I can't help thinking that this is now my life. There will always be an empty chair where you should be.

Everyone who loves me thinks it will be easier if I am with family or friends for the holidays. I wish that were true, but it doesn't seem to make much difference. I have just returned from spending several days with Don and Melba (my brother and his wife) over Thanksgiving. They were extra-attentive, gracious, and kind. Although I enjoyed their company, it didn't make me miss you any less. In fact, I might have missed you more. Whether we were eating together, or playing table games, or just reminiscing about holidays past, your chair was always empty, a sad reminder that you are gone.

On Thursday I will drive to New York to spend Christmas with Doug, Leah, and Deuce. You would be proud of Leah. She has been working so hard to make this Christmas extra-special for me. She's baked all my favorite desserts, planned the holiday menu to cater to my tastes, set up a small office where I can write, and decorated the house to the nines! I feel greatly loved, but without you, nothing else really matters. I can't imagine what Christmas will be like since you won't be there.

My birthday is just a couple of days away and this will be the first birthday I have spent without you in nearly sixty years. Although you were a perfectionist and the consummate "detail person," you couldn't remember birthdays—not your mother's, not your sister's, not even mine. Every year on December 16th, the telephone would ring early in the morning. I always answered it, and when I did, Dad and Mom would sing "Happy Birthday." After I hung up the phone, you would glare at me and ask, "Is today your birthday?"

I would grin and reply, "It's December sixteenth, so it must be my birthday. Happens on this day every year!"

About twenty years ago, you told me that if I failed to remind you of my birthday ever again, you were going to kill me. I don't think you meant that literally, but I wasn't taking any chances, so each year, about a week before my birthday, I started telling you, "In one week, I will have a birthday." A couple days later, "Friday is my birthday." And then, "Tomorrow is my birthday." Well, baby girl, I just want to remind you that Friday is my birthday. I sure wish we could spend it together.

Alexia (our granddaughter) misses you almost as much as I do. She has one huge regret. On the Tuesday evening before you passed, you asked her to spend the night at the hospice facility with us. It was late—nearly midnight, I think—and she had to work the next day, so she reluctantly declined. She bid you goodnight promising to return as soon as she got off work the next evening. You hugged her neck and whispered, "I won't be here when you get back tomorrow."

How did you know?

When Alexia and I were having dinner together a few days ago, I told her I didn't think I would ever get over your death. She reached across the table and squeezed my hand. "Grief," she said, "is like a rubber ball, maybe the size of a tennis ball or a softball. Our life is like a glass into which that rubber ball has been shoved. Initially it totally fills the glass, forcing everything else out. Over time, things change. Although your grief never diminishes, your life expands, making room for love and laughter and joy again."

That's maybe the best explanation I have ever heard, and she's just twenty-two years old. How did she become so wise?

I sure hope she's right, because right now my life is filled to the brim with grief. My faith is strong, but my emotions are all over the place, and it only takes the mention of your name, or a favorite song, or a poignant memory to cause my throat to get tight and my eyes to tear up. Right now, it seems all the light has gone out of my life, and it feels like I am wandering in the dark, but I am not alone. Jesus is with me!

With all my love forever,

THE FIFTH LETTER

You are my hiding place;
you will protect me from trouble
and surround me with songs of
deliverance.

PSALMS 32:7 NIV

Dearest Brenda:

I've never believed in Murphy's Law—"Anything that can go wrong will go wrong"—but I'm starting to. When I returned home after spending Thanksgiving with Don and Melba in Texas, I discovered a water leak had ruined the hardwood floors in the master bathroom. I didn't have time to get the leak fixed before heading to New York for Christmas with Leah, so I simply shut off the water at the pressure tank. On Thursday morning, when I got into the car to leave, it wouldn't start. I called AAA, and they towed it into the Buick dealership in Fayetteville. I ended up spending all day sitting in the lounge next to the showroom waiting for them to get the car repaired. The mechanic discovered that squirrels had built a nest on the engine and chewed the wires in two. Unbelievable! I had only left it out of the garage one night. Like I was saying: "Anything that can go wrong will go wrong."

In the past, I would have been extremely frustrated, maybe even angry. Not now. Since your death, nothing seems to matter much. Compared to losing you, what are ruined hardwood floors or a car that won't start? Just little hangnails. Inconvenient, to be sure, and costly, but that's all.

It was dark the next morning when I closed up the house and climbed into the car to leave for New York. I was blinking back tears as I eased down the quarter-mile track leading to Angell Road before turning right and heading for the highway seven miles away. I couldn't help thinking that just last year, we had made this trip together, never imagining for a minute that it would be the last time. We knew there was a possibility the cancer would return, but we never dreamed it would happen so soon or that it would be so deadly.

The day I left for New York was my seventy-sixth birthday, and the first one I have spent without you in over sixty years. To keep from breaking down, I forced myself to remember the special birthdays we spent together. There was my twenty-ninth birthday in Craig, Colorado. You bought me a beautiful blue-and-white sweater with a hood and baked me a butter brickle birthday cake—my favorite. That's the year I started growing my beard, and I've had it ever since. A lot of men have beards now, but at the time it was pretty radical, especially for a pastor.

You made a big deal out of my fortieth birthday. We lived in Tulsa, and we were serving as the pastors of Christian Chapel. You invited several of my closest friends to meet us at the Rafters restaurant for a birthday dinner. To top it off, Leah surprised me by bringing several of her friends from the Union High School choir to the restaurant to sing "Happy Birthday" to me. What a special night that was!

Despite my determination not to think about your death, my mind has a will of its own, and it keeps returning to your last days in the hospice facility. Our first morning there, while the hospice doctor was making the arrangements to have the fluid drained from your abdomen a second time, you said, "I don't think I can do this again."

Taking your hand, I held it next to my cheek and said, "You don't have to. It might make you more comfortable, but it's not going to prolong your life."

I was weeping as I said it because I knew you were choosing to die. You had no unfinished business, not with the Lord, not with me, and not with Leah or your grandchildren. You were ready to go home. You had fought the good fight, finished your race, and kept the faith. Now you were eager to hear Jesus say, "Well done, good and faithful servant!" (Matthew 25:21 NIV).

Leah and Deuce arrived shortly thereafter for a final visit before flying home to enroll him in college. As their time with you was drawing to a close, Deuce invited me to join him in the chapel for prayer. When we finished praying, I began quoting the words to one of our favorite hymns, "What a Day That Will Be." As soon as we got back to your room, Deuce went on YouTube and found it. Soon the sounds of that glorious hymn filled the room, and you raised your hands to Jesus and started singing.

I was amazed. You had your voice back!

Before your brain surgery, four years earlier, you'd had a voice like Anne Murray. Following surgery, your voice was raspy, and you struggled to stay on pitch. A lot of other things changed, as well. You lost your sense of smell, you struggled with short-term memory, and your personality changed, but nothing was more dramatic than the loss of your ability to sing. Now you were singing the way I remembered, and when Leah began harmonizing with you, my heart soared.

Too soon the song ended, and unbidden tears flooded my eyes as I watched you hug them tightly as they bid you goodbye. I can't even imagine what you must have been feeling, knowing this was the last time you would ever see them or hold them close in this life. Little did I know that in only forty-eight hours, you would be bidding all of us goodbye as you left this world for a better place. Knowing you are with Jesus, in the place He has prepared for you, where there is no more sickness or death, is the only thing that enables me to face each new day.

The trip to New York was grueling. I drove seven hundred miles the first day before exhaustion forced me to stop. I wanted to keep going, but it was pitch-black and sleeting, making it difficult for me to see the highway. And Murphy's Law struck again. The last time I'd had the car serviced, someone had filled the windshield washer reservoir with plain water rather than washer fluid, and now it was frozen. Every time a truck or car passed me, my windshield was plastered with dirty slush, making it nearly impossible for me to see. I tried using the windshield wipers, but that just made it worse. Finally, I stopped for the night at a no-name motel.

Had you been with me we would have stopped hours earlier, like we did last year. Four hundred miles a day was your limit. In my mind's eye, I can see you in our hotel room sitting on the bed in your pajamas engrossed in a TV show—probably something on a shopping channel or a cooking show. Of course, I would have been reading a book on my Kindle. That was last year, and that's why I didn't stop earlier. I couldn't bear the thought of spending several hours in a hotel room without you. I was determined to drive as long as possible in the hopes that when I finally got a room, I would be so exhausted I would simply pass out.

It didn't work. Although my body ached with fatigue and my eyes burned with exhaustion, sleep escaped me. I tossed and turned, trying to find a comfortable position on an unfamiliar bed. Finally, I gave up and embraced the memories that were wooing me. They were bittersweet, promising comfort, but even the happiest memories soon morphed into memories of your suffering and death. I can't help but wonder if it will always be like this. Will every good memory always be tainted by memories of your suffering and death? The grief recovery books tell me that in time, the painful memories will fade, to be replaced by the joyous memories of the rich life we lived. I hope they are right because the pain of losing you is nearly killing me.

With all my love forever,

Richard

P.S. A few days ago, I was sitting in my recliner in the living room listening to music. My iPod was connected to the Bose system, and "our songs"—the ones we've been listening to since we bought our first stereo way back in 1968—carried me back to an earlier, happier time. Almost every song brought back a memory, and I found myself reliving our life together. My nostalgic journey was interrupted when an unfamiliar song filled the room. In an instant, I was transfixed. Dolly Parton and Ricky Van Shelton were singing our love story. Yes, our love story! How had I missed it? It was on my iPod. I must have heard it before, probably countless times, but it had never registered until now. They were singing about being friends and lovers—from first love through the birth of babies to old age, what they called "our rockin' years." See why I call it our love song?

THE SIXTH LETTER

Love is invincible facing danger and death.
Passion laughs at the terrors of hell.
The fire of love stops at nothing—
it sweeps everything before it.
Flood waters can't drown love,
torrents of rain can't put it out.

SONG OF SOLOMON 8:6–7 MSG

Dearest Brenda:

It is the day after Christmas, and I am looking out Leah's kitchen window at a boy and girl ice-skating on a frozen pond. The temperature is barely above zero, with a wind-chill factor considerably colder, yet they seem unaware of the cold as they cavort together on the ice. I envy them. They are young, and if they are not in love, they are at least strongly attracted to each other. We were once like that, so much in love that we were oblivious to the heat or the cold, risking sunburn or frostbite to spend time together. Do you remember the August afternoon we spent swimming in the South Platte River while ignoring the sun's deadly rays? Or the time we went ice-skating on a frozen pond swept clean of snow by frigid winds high in the Rockies? I would give almost anything if we could do it again, but that will never happen.

It's been four months and one day since you departed this world for a better place. I'm tempted to calculate how many days, hours, and minutes it has been since you took your last breath, but with a determined effort I refuse to go there. Although my grief is still raw, I am determined to remember the good times we shared. Your brain surgery and your battle with uterine cancer were a part of our life, but that's all—just a part. With God's help, I am determined to remember the life we lived—all of it—not just your death.

One of my favorite memories is of the Christmas we spent with Bud and Joyce in a cabin near Monarch Pass, high in the Colorado Rockies. We laughed and talked while playing table games and feasting on Christmas goodies. The next morning dawned clear and cold—*really* cold—with the temperatures in the single digits. Bud and Joyce chose to stay inside by the fire rather than risk the frigid temperatures, but we bundled up, grabbed our ice skates, and headed for the frozen pond behind the cabin.

Even now, these many years later, I can picture that morning in my mind as clearly as if it just happened yesterday. Leah was only four years old and hadn't yet learned to skate, but she insisted on following us onto the ice. She was wearing snow boots and a dark brown coat with a hood, trimmed with fake fur, the doll she got for Christmas grasped by one arm. As always, you were stylish and beautiful, your eyes sparkling as you gracefully skated around the pond. I followed close behind, never taking my eyes off you. The love that nearly caused my heart to burst that December morning in 1974 still burns in my heart today and always will.

I live alone now, and the winter nights are long and dark this time of the year. When you were here, that never bothered me; in fact, I welcomed the coming of the night. We loved sitting by the wood-burning stove with only a kerosene lamp for light, listening to music and reminiscing about our life together. Now it seems the night will never end, and I wonder if it will always be like this. I'm tempted to feel sorry for myself, but again, I refuse to go there. Instead, I boot up my computer and open the photo app, thankful once again for all the hours you and I spent scanning photos from our early years. I've made several albums on my computer—family, friends, Emerald Pointe, Alexia and Deuce, Doug and Leah, and of course, an album for us.

I open "our" album and begin scrolling through the years, paying particular attention to the ministry photos.

I'm looking at pictures of us when we were just kids, serving as the pastors of the Assembly of God in Holly, Colorado. I was only twenty years old, and you were a year younger. In the first picture, we are standing beside the church sign. You are wearing a white skirt, a yellow-and-white blouse, and yellow sandals. Of course, I'm wearing a suit and tie. Across the bottom of the sign is the motto: "You're Never a Stranger in Your Father's House." In a second photo, we are sitting in my office. I am talking on the telephone, and you are typing on the small, portable typewriter I used to type my sermons. In another, I am squatting in the snow beside the church making a snowball. There are several more, and each one evokes a poignant memory.

It still amazes me that you, a city girl from Houston, were not only willing, but eager to follow me to a tiny town in extreme southeastern Colorado. Colorful Colorado it wasn't! The congregation was small, numbering less than twenty congregants, with nearly everyone old enough to be our grandparents. The parsonage was old and in poor repair, but none of that bothered you. You were absolutely fearless. You embraced the challenges and hardships without flinching. Thinking about it now, more than fifty years later, I can only marvel at your resilience. The only thing you ever complained about was going to the Laundromat. You hated that!

Here's a picture of the groundbreaking service for the church in Craig, Colorado, and several photos of the new church building we built in 1979–1980. Can you believe my hair was that long? In this photo, the three of us (Leah, you, and me) are walking through Christian Chapel's building when it was under construction, something we did almost every Saturday morning. Afterward we would meet Ben and Rochelle at What-A-Burger for lunch. In the next photo, I'm preaching at the huge pro-life rally at the State Capitol in Oklahoma City. According to my recollection, there were fourteen thousand people in attendance, but both you and Leah remembered twenty thousand. Whatever the number, it was impressive.

You always believed in me, and you were willing to follow me wherever the Lord was leading—be it a tiny church in Holly, Colorado, or a struggling congregation in Tulsa, Oklahoma, or a church in crisis in Shreveport, Louisiana. You always supported me in whatever ministry I felt the Lord was calling us to—be it writing books, or doing radio, or traveling as itinerant ministers, or risking arrest in front of an abortion mill. You never tried to hold me back or resisted my spiritual leadership.

The closest you ever came was when the official board from Gateway Church in Shreveport telephoned and asked me if I would consider interviewing for the senior pastor position. I told them I would pray about it and get back to them. When I ended the call, you said, "You're not *really* going to pray about that, are you?" When I said I was, you burst into tears. I quickly assured you that I wouldn't consider accepting that position unless the Lord confirmed it to your heart also. Not surprisingly, He did, and two days later, you said, "If you feel the Lord wants us to go to Shreveport, I'm onboard."

I spent several hours looking at pictures chronicling our past. Although I had to blink back tears on several occasions, I could only conclude that the life we shared was rich, indeed, and wonderfully blessed by the Lord. In one way, all the memories only make me miss you more, but in another way, I am comforted. As long as I have these memories, you will live on in my heart.

Although I have no idea what my immediate future looks like, God's faithfulness throughout our life and ministry gives me confidence to face it without fear. And when my own life on earth is over, I am confident that Jesus will come for me, and we will spend eternity together in His presence. "Even so, come, Lord Jesus" (Revelation 22:20 KJV).

Thank you, Brenda Starr, for the memories.

With all my love forever,

Richard

THE SEVENTH LETTER

Praise be to the God and Father of our Lord Jesus Christ,
the Father of compassion and the God of all comfort,
who comforts us in all our troubles.

2 CORINTHIANS 1:3–4 NIV

Dearest Brenda:

Although I have ministered to countless grieving people, I'm still amazed at how much I didn't know. Thankfully I was wise enough not to make some of the inane comments people have made to me—things like, "I know what you're feeling. I lost my grandmother last year." Or, "You should be thankful you had so many years together. Cancer took my husband before our twenty-fifth anniversary." I know they mean well, so I try not to let their comments upset me, but I can tell you they provide no comfort.

I shared some of my grief journey while speaking at a minister's meeting some weeks ago. Following my message, a young woman approached me with tears glistening in her eyes. Hesitantly she asked, "May I give you a hug?" If a picture is worth a thousand words, then that hug was priceless. If only more people could understand that a hug, or an arm around the shoulders, or some other appropriate touch is worth more than all the words ever spoken.

Maybe that's what I miss most—your touch. I loved holding your hand, whether we were walking our property or sitting in the rocking chairs on the boat dock or lying in bed at night. I will never forget holding your hand for the very first time, sitting in the dark on Halloween night, while Linda (your sister) told ghost stories. And I will never forget the last time I held your hand as you took your final breath.

Immediately following your death, while I was driving home from the Circle of Life hospice facility, I was blindsided by the tempter. For the first time in my life, I found myself doubting the reality of eternal life. I was overwhelmed with the fear that I would never see you again, that when you took your last breath, you ceased to exist. I know that sounds crazy, but at the time, it was terrifyingly real. I can only conclude that grief concusses our emotions, leaving us disoriented and susceptible to thoughts and feelings to which we would ordinarily be immune.

Although my emotions were all over the place, the truth of God's Word became my anchor. During my prayer time, I quoted the Scriptures about eternal life again and again.[1] As I did, my confidence was restored, and I comforted myself with the knowledge that one day we will be together again.

On our fiftieth anniversary, you wanted to hire a professional photographer to take pictures to commemorate the occasion. Although I was tempted to protest, saying it was too expensive, I'm so thankful I had sense enough to agree. I treasure those photos now and spend hours looking at them. After the photo shoot, I took you to Ruth's Chris Steak House. I surprised you by asking the maître d' if could speak with the chef. When he came to our table, I told him I didn't want to look at the menu. Instead, I ask him to prepare the best meal possible—appetizers, entrée, and dessert. You just sat there in amazement, unable to believe I was being so

---

[1] "I (Jesus) am the resurrection, and the life: he that believeth in me, though he were dead, yet shall he live" (John 11:25 KJV). "In my Father's house are many mansions: if it were not so, I would have told you. I go to prepare a place for you. And if I go and prepare a place for you, I will come again, and receive you unto myself; that where I am, there ye may be also" (John 14:2–3 KJV). To be absent from the body is to be present with Christ. (see 2 Corinthians 5:8). "For me to live is Christ, and to die is gain" (Philippians 1:21 KJV). "I desire to depart and be with Christ, which is better by far" (Philippians 1:23 NIV).

recklessly extravagant. The meal was spectacular, but the best part was your joy!

Last year I wanted to take you back to Ruth's Chris for our fifty-sixth anniversary. We invited Brandon and Alexia to be our guests, as they were celebrating their first anniversary. Of course, we would have to order off the menu. I can only be recklessly extravagant once every fifty years! When we went online and looked at the menu, we decided we couldn't afford it. Instead, we settled for a less-expensive steakhouse. Bad mistake. The meal was just passable, and it still cost almost two hundred dollars for the four of us. Had I known that was the last anniversary you and I would ever celebrate together on this earth, you better believe I would have taken you to Ruth's Chris Steak House or somewhere even better—and we wouldn't have ordered off the menu, either.

A few days before you died, we were sitting on the porch overlooking the lake. I could tell you had something on your mind, so I sat quietly waiting for you to speak. Finally, you said, "Don't say no until you hear me out." You paused, waiting for me to respond, so I nodded. When I did, you continued, "When you sell Emerald Pointe, I want you to use some of the proceeds to finish renovating Doug and Leah's house. Then I want you to help Alexia and Brandon with a down payment so they can buy a house. I also want you to help pay for Deuce's college."

I agreed, although I had serious doubts there would be enough money to do all that, plus buy a small house where I could live out my days. I will not forget your final request, of that you may be sure, and I will do everything in my power to honor it. I can't help thinking you faced death the way you lived life—thinking of others before yourself. I can only marvel at your selflessness.

Your opening statement—"Don't say no until you hear me out"—grieved me. That one comment told me more than I wanted to know. Apparently I had said "no" far too often during our fifty-six years of marriage. With a heavy heart, I recall how often I said we couldn't afford it when you wanted to go to a show in Branson. When you wanted to drive through Eureka Springs looking at the houses for the hundredth time, I declined, saying I was too tired. I'm ashamed of how many times I tried to discourage you when you wanted to buy a new outfit from the Home Shopping Network or jewelry from QVC. So what, if you had a closet full of clothes and more jewelry than I could imagine? I wish I could go back and do it again. Surely I would do better.

When we left the oncologist's office for the last time, just six days before you died, you wanted to get something to eat. I'm ashamed to admit I was tempted to say, "Let's just go home. We have plenty of food at the house." Besides, I knew you couldn't eat more than three or four bites, so why bother? Thank God I didn't say something stupid like that out loud. Instead, I drove to Panda Express (one of your favorites) and ordered takeout because you were too weak to go inside. You were so tired I decided to drive home while you ate. Of course, two or three bites was all you could manage. My heart was breaking when you started feeding me honey walnut shrimp while I drove. I couldn't help thinking that it would probably be the last time you would ever do anything like that—and it was. Two days later, an ambulance transported you to the Circle of Life hospice facility in Bentonville, a trip from which you never returned.

Since your death, I am often tempted with regret. I wish I had said "yes" more often, but I comfort myself with the knowledge that we made a lot of good memories—ski trips to Colorado, vacations to Yellowstone and Glacier National parks, Lake Tahoe and Canada, California and Hawaii. One of my favorite memories is the European trip we took with John and Ruth. We visited the Netherlands, Germany, and Austria. When we returned to Brussels, we went to the Grand Place after dark. After a walking tour taking in the sights, we turned down a side street and stepped into a small Greek café, where we ordered gyros. The guy shaving the lamb for our gyros flirted shamelessly, never taking his eyes off you. I was tempted to crawl across the counter and poke a stick in his eye, but he had that sharp knife, so I restrained myself. I did have the last laugh, though. I smirked at him as I walked away with my arm around your waist!

There are so many memories, and each one is bitter-sweet. Sweet because they allow me to relive the life we shared. For instance, I remember doing devotions together early each morning while sitting beside the wood-burning stove at Emerald Pointe. I remember how you used to bring me a steaming cup of French-pressed coffee when I had been writing for hours. At the end of the day, I remember reading to you and how you would rave about what I had written, especially my novels. But the memories are bitter, too. Bitter because now I have no one to read to, no one to rave about what I've written or give me helpful suggestions. Bitter because when I shut out the light and crawl into bed each night, there is no goodnight kiss, no holding hands for a final nighttime prayer, no one to say, "I love you, too," when I whisper, "I love you," into the darkness. Now all I have are the memories, and although they give me a measure of comfort, when I think of spending the rest of my life alone, without you, I am undone.

The loneliness is nearly more than I can bear, but my faith remains strong. I take hope because the psalmist said, "Weeping may last through the night, but joy comes with the morning. . . . You (Lord) have turned my mourning into joyful dancing. You have taken away my clothes of mourning and clothed me with joy" (Psalm 30:5, 11 NLT). I can't help wondering how long the night of my grief will last, how long before my mourning will be turned into dancing.

With all my love forever,

THE EIGHTH LETTER

Behold, God is my salvation,
I will trust and not be afraid;
For the LORD GOD is my strength and song,
And He has become my salvation."

ISAIAH 12:2 NASB

Dearest Brenda:

It was dark when I turned into the driveway in front of our house at Emerald Pointe following two hard days on the road. After spending the holidays with Leah (our daughter) and her family in upstate New York, I was eager to get home, but I dreaded coming home to an empty house. In times past, the light would have been on, and you would have met me on the front porch with open arms and a "welcome home" kiss. Not this time, nor ever again. Just before dawn, on a Thursday morning nearly five months ago, you departed this life. I should be getting used to the idea of living alone, but I'm not. I keep hoping this is just a bad dream and that I will wake up and reach across the bed and touch you. In my saner moments, I know that's not going to happen, but I keep hoping.

The two-day trip from upstate New York nearly wiped me out–not physically, but emotionally. Too much time to think, I guess. I couldn't help thinking that I had missed so many clues. I don't know what I could have done differently, but I should have been more perceptive. I should have realized how sick you were when you spent so much time lying in bed. I should have realized how weak you were when you asked for a wheelchair when we went to the hospital to have your abdomen drained. When we visited the oncologist for the last time, you laid down on a couch in the waiting room, too weak to sit up, but I still didn't get it. Nor did I realize the end was just five days away when the oncologist ordered hospice care. Your father lived six more weeks after he began hospice care. I guess that was what I was expecting.

The clues seem so obvious in retrospect. Although they drained your abdomen on Monday, by Friday it was so swollen you had difficulty breathing. That should have told me something, but I didn't get it. Maybe I was in denial. Once you entered the Circle of Life hospice facility, you didn't eat anything. On Monday morning, you ordered Malt-O-Meal with lots of butter and sugar, just the way you like it, but you didn't take a single bite. I peeled an orange for you, but when you tasted it, you spit it out, saying it was too sweet. How did I miss that? Nothing was ever too sweet for you.

When Frank and Linda arrived from Oklahoma City, Linda came bearing gifts like she always did. She gave you a beautiful bracelet with an intricate design. You looked at it but couldn't make out the detail. I handed you your reading glasses, but they didn't help. Another clue. Your vision was failing. For three days, you had a steady stream of visitors, friends from across the country coming to express their love. You responded warmly, taking pleasure in their presence, but you said very little. I should have known your body was shutting down, but I didn't realize it. You were always the quiet one, listening more than talking, so your quietness didn't seem all that unusual.

Because I missed the clues, because I didn't realize what was happening until it was too late, I didn't get a chance to tell you goodbye. I stepped out of your room for just a minute to call Leah, and in an instant, you lost consciousness. Although you lingered through the night, you never regained consciousness. I never left your bedside. I prayed the Scriptures and quoted the great hymns of the faith, but I don't think I told you how much I loved you. Maybe I did. I hope I did, but I have no clear recollection. How could I have let you slip into eternity without saying, "I love you"? I said it every day of our married life, sometimes several times a day. Surely I told you how much I loved you during the last hours you spent on this earth, but I have no memory of it, and it grieves me. If I didn't, it was only because my grief had rendered me mute.

I wish I had asked our friends to step out of the room for a few minutes before you lost consciousness so we could have had some time alone. It wasn't that we had any unfinished business. We didn't. We had already said all there was to say. Not just in recent days, but again and again, over the years. You thanked me for giving you back your life, and I thanked you for forgiving me for the anger that had wounded you so deeply in our early years. I thanked you for always loving me, and you thanked me for laying down my life for our family. I told you that you were the light of my life and my greatest joy. You said I was your lifeline and your hero. Poignant words, heavy with the love of a lifetime, but still not large enough to express the love that overflowed our hearts.

Instead of asking our friends to give us a few minutes alone, I let you slip into eternity without thanking you one last time for the wonderful life you made for me. I didn't get to tell you that you are my favorite person in the whole world and the most beautiful woman I have ever seen. I wanted to tell you that coming home to you was the highlight of every day, that I appreciated how you always took great pains to look your best. I wanted to thank you one last time for how special you made our home, for all the winter evenings when you had a fire in the fireplace, the table set with candles and cloth napkins, and a well-prepared meal ready to be served. Truly you made our home this man's castle, and I will always be in your debt.

Like I said, I wish I had asked our friends to step out of the room for a few minutes, but I didn't, and now it is too late.

The thing about death is that it is so final. There is nothing, absolutely nothing, any of us can do to rescind it. We are utterly powerless to undo the terrible thing it has done. Never have I felt so helpless, so impotent. Heretofore anytime I suffered a devastating setback, or a crushing disappointment, I knew that, with God's help, I could turn things around. Death is different. No matter how hard I pray, no matter how much faith I have, I'm not going to undo what death has done. You are gone, and you're not coming back. How did David say it when his infant son died? "But now he is dead. Why should I fast? Can I bring him back again? *I shall go to him, but he will not return to me*" (2 Samuel 12:23 ESV, emphasis added).

To my surprise, I've discovered the valley of the shadow of death is a haunted place. Old hurts, which I thought were healed long ago, have come back to torment me. Painful memories ambush me, memories I thought were dead and buried. This dark place forces me to admit that no one goes through life unscathed, and no marriage is perfect. The sad truth is, we all sin against our marriage; in small ways and not-so-small ways, we all hurt the one we love, the one we never meant to hurt at all. It pains me in ways I can't even describe to know I hurt you. What was I thinking? How could I have been so selfish? And you hurt me, wounded me in ways no one else ever has or ever could. Yet for all that, our marriage weathered the storm. By God's grace, it not only survived, but it became all the Lord intended marriage to be. Forgiveness was given and received. Our love was renewed, a deeper, more selfless love.

Yet now, as I walk through this dark place, this valley of the shadow of death, I am suddenly accosted by painful memories I haven't thought of in decades. Like rabid jackals, they rip and tear at me, threatening to destroy every good memory. These old hurts tempt me to relive past failures, to doubt every positive memory, to question the truth of my life, but I refuse to go there. "There is now no condemnation for those who are in Christ Jesus" (Romans 8:1 NIV). With determined deliberateness, I exercise the disciplines of a lifetime, I take captive every evil imagination and make every memory, every thought, obedient to Christ (see 2 Corinthians 10:3–5).

I take hope because I am not alone in this dark place, never alone. The Lord is with me, and His rod and His staff comfort me. When the enemy tries to overwhelm me with the bitter memories of past failures, He anoints my head with oil, healing the old hurts, renewing my mind. He prepares a table of grace before me, renewing my soul, and He restores the memories of the love we shared and the rich life we lived. Surely His goodness and His mercy will follow me all the days of my life, and we—you and I—will dwell together in the house of the Lord forever (see Psalm 23).

I wasn't surprised when grief caused me to question what kind of life I would have without you, to wonder if I would ever be happy again, to wonder if the things that once brought me joy—reading a good book, listening to music, visiting with old friends, writing—would ever bring me joy again. I expected that. What I didn't expect was that grief would make me question my core beliefs, like the reality of eternal life. Immediately following your death, I was assailed with an overwhelming fear that when you took your last breath, you ceased to exist. I feared I would never see you again. Nor did I expect grief to tempt me to relive old hurts, but it did. It does. Like I've said before, I can only conclude that grief concusses our emotions, leaving us disoriented and susceptible to thoughts and feelings to which we would ordinarily be immune.

In light of that, I'm thankful for a lifetime of spiritual disciplines, for they are what sustain me now in the hour of my grief. Memorized Scriptures shore up my soul and refute the lies of the enemy. The practice of prayer renews my mind and strengthens my inner being. Holy communion cleanses and heals me, feeding my soul. Worship, both public and private, nourishes my faith, as does fellowship with the body of Christ. These disciplines we practiced together as husband and wife. They gave you faith to face death without fear. Now these same disciplines give me faith to live without you, knowing that one day soon I, too, will depart this life for a better place, where there is no more sickness or death. We will meet again to never part. Of that I am totally convinced.

With all my love forever,

Richard

P.S. A few days after you died, John Merrell and I were sitting on the glider overlooking the lake, the beauty of God's creation only marred by the grief that was choking me and blinding my eyes with tears. He fiddled with his iPhone for a minute, and then Guy Penrod's voice washed over us in healing waves. As he sang, "Knowing What I Know About

Heaven," I was enveloped by grace, God's amazing grace. My heart was still breaking, but the lyrics turned my wordless sorrow into praise. As much as I love you, and as empty as my life is without you, I wouldn't bring you back, even if I could. Knowing what I know about heaven, why on earth would I do that?

THE NINTH LETTER

*Tell those who mourn that the time of God's favor to
them has come. . . .
To all who mourn in Israel he will give: beauty for ashes;
joy instead of mourning; praise instead of heaviness.*

ISAIAH 61:2–3 TLB

Dearest Brenda:

It's been nearly three weeks since my last letter. Several
times I've sat down to write, but I just didn't have the heart
for it. It's now been five months since you left me for a better
place, and if anything, my grief is worse than ever. Not a day
goes by but what I find myself weeping for you. When I sit
by the wood-burning stove in the early morning darkness,
and I hear the dog coming to join me, for just a moment I
think it might be you. I call into the darkness, "Baby girl,

is that you?" I know it's not you, but still, for an instant, I think this whole grief thing might just be a bad dream.

Yesterday would have been your seventy-fifth birthday. Instead of celebrating it here with me, you spent it rejoicing with Jesus. Lucky girl! You loved birthdays, anyone's—mine, Leah's, your grandchildren's, your mother's, and your friends. Two years ago, we celebrated your seventy-third birthday at the Grotto Wood-Fired Grill and Wine Cave in Eureka Springs with Alexia and Brandon. Last year, you were grieving your mother's passing and recovering from COVID, so we didn't do anything special, but you still got your birthday cake. Had I known it would be the last birthday we would ever spend together on this earth, I would have found a way to make it special, no matter what.

As you know, I'm not nearly as good at planning special celebrations as you were, but I think I outdid myself for your fiftieth birthday. I surprised you by flying Linda (your sister) in from Houston. The three of us went to the movie theater, where we saw *Titanic*, and then we went to Charleston's for lunch. Later, a host of friends helped me give you a surprise birthday party on the sixtieth floor of the Citiplex Towers in Tulsa. Following the party, we spent the night in the spacious penthouse on the fifty-ninth floor. All in all, it was truly a spectacular birthday!

Twenty years later, for your seventieth birthday, I asked family and friends to send you cards and letters expressing their love and appreciation. When they arrived, Alexia and I placed them in vinyl sleeves before putting them in a three-ring notebook. In addition, I scanned several photos—beginning with your baby pictures and continuing through the fifty-plus years of our life together. After enlarging them, I printed them and put them in the purple notebook with the letters from your dearest friends. Yesterday I spent the entire morning rereading those letters and looking at the photos. It wasn't like having you here, but it was the best I could do.

I posted some of the photos and excerpts from the letters on Facebook, and the response was incredible. More than a hundred people responded with scores of people wishing you a happy birthday in heaven. To read their outpouring of love and appreciation for you was heartwarming. It was almost like a surprise birthday party. I must confess, I had a little trouble imagining celebrating birthdays in heaven, where time does not exist. Be that as it may, I still enjoyed reading their expressions of love for you.

I have now been home from New York for three weeks. That's the longest time I have spent alone at Emerald Pointe since you went to be with Jesus. I love being here, but I have never felt so alone. I'm not lonely. I'm alone! There's a difference. If I were just lonely, I would meet a friend in town for lunch or go visit family. That would fix the loneliness, but

I would still be alone. Only you can fix this aloneness, and you're not coming back.

Little did I realize what we were doing when we bought these six acres on this remote part of Beaver Lake in 1991. The fact that it was nine miles to the nearest paved road and twenty-five miles to the nearest grocery store seemed idyllic to us. Carroll Electric Cooperative brought power to the property. Subsequently, we drilled a well and put in a septic system. The first two years we were without telephone service or television. It was almost like going back in time. On long winter evenings, we read by the wood-burning stove, played table games, or just talked. Sometimes we chatted with only a kerosene lamp for light in memory of my grandma Miller. Not once did I feel isolated or alone.

It's different now. I still love the solitude, but I now realize the risks of living alone so far from everyone. As you know, my closest family members, except for Alexia and her husband, who live an hour away, are hundreds of miles away. I now understand why you said if I died before you, you wouldn't stay here, not for a single night. I get it. Although you were never lonely when I was here with you, living alone here is altogether different, as I am learning.

I often prayed, asking the Lord to let me live at least one day longer than you. I never wanted you to face the aloneness and grief that I'm living with now that you're gone. As I have learned during this ordeal, you are a remarkably strong person, stronger than I could have ever imagined given your gentle disposition. I have no doubt that you could handle the grief at least as well as I am, but still, I'm so thankful you will never have to. Even if I could, I would never bring you back. At last, you are free from all pain and sorrow. God Himself has wiped away your tears. Everlasting joy is yours!

Some people say there is just a thin veil between this life and the next. They say they can sense their departed loved one's near presence. That hasn't been my experience. I wander through the house, from room to room, admiring the artistic way you decorated, but I don't sense your presence. Even though I see your fingerprints everywhere, you're not here. I spend hours looking at photos of our life together, but as much as I enjoy the memories, you are still gone, and I am alone—more alone than I have ever been. I don't think anyone can understand the depth of this aloneness until they lose their spouse.

Never again will I hear you singing a favorite song as you fix your hair. Never again will I hear your joyous laughter as you talk with Leah or your sister on the phone. Never again will I see you dancing in the living room as you sway to one of "our" songs—maybe "Look at Us" or "Back Home Again." Never again will we sit by the wood-burning stove sharing devotions in the predawn darkness. Never again will we enjoy coffee together sweetened with thick country cream. Never again will we sit together on the porch watching the harvest moon come up over the lake. Never again will we hold hands and share a final prayer before drifting toward sleep. Never again . . . On these long, lonely nights, I'm haunted by a hundred or more "never again"s.

Still, having said that, I choose to give the Lord a sacrifice of praise. I will praise Him for the lifetime of love we shared. I will praise Him for His near presence. I will praise Him for the promise of eternal life. And I will praise Him that one day soon, we will be reunited to spend eternity together in His presence, where there is no more sorrow or death.

With all my love forever,

THE TENTH LETTER

Don't panic. I'm with you.
There's no need to fear for I'm your God.
I'll give you strength. I'll help you.
I'll hold you steady, keep a firm grip on you.
I'm not letting go.
I'm telling you, "Don't panic.
I'm right here to help you."

ISAIAH 41:10, 13 MSG

Dearest Brenda:

I knew I would grieve following your death, but I had no idea the many forms it would take or how overwhelming it would be. The physical toll blindsided me, upsetting my digestive system and making sleep nearly impossible. Within a few days, stress pinched a nerve in my neck, causing a burning pain to shoot into the back of my upper arm, through my elbow, and into the tips of my fingers. I couldn't extend my arm or lift it over my head without severe pain. I saw a neurosurgeon, had an MRI, and underwent chiropractic treatments, massage therapy, and acupuncture. After two months, I was considerably better, but even now, almost six months after your death, I still deal with pain every day.

My interest in life waned. I tried to read but discovered most books couldn't keep my attention. Weeks went by before I turned on the TV. Even now I can't bring myself to watch the programs we enjoyed together. Although I've been an avid sports fan all my life, I now find the games boring beyond belief. I couldn't even get excited when the Houston Astros won the World Series. I couldn't help remembering that we had watched it together the last time they won. Watching it without you just wasn't the same. I tried to watch the NFL playoffs, but I ended up sleeping through most of the games. Not even my first deer hunt in more than forty years excited me, although it was nice to hunt with Don (my brother).

Friends and family are determined to help me through the most difficult days. They invite me to spend the holidays with them and to come for extended visits, which I am doing. Spending time with them is helpful, but it does not alleviate my grief. No matter who I am with, I am still alone. Thankfully my faith remains strong, but going to church requires a herculean effort. Worshiping the Lord was something we always did together, and it is not the same without you.

It seems each day I realize another way in which my life is diminished without you. You did so many things amazingly well and without ever drawing attention to yourself. As you know, we sent flowers to the funerals of several friends. Each time I asked you to take care of it, and then I never gave it a second thought. I knew the flowers you sent would be perfect. You told the florist exactly what flowers you wanted and the colors.

How did you know the names of all those flowers? You weren't a florist. You never had any training in horticulture, so how did you do that? I guess I just assumed it was an innate knowledge all women were born with. Boy, was I wrong. When I tried to order a floral arrangement for your memorial service, I quickly realized I was out of my league. Leah couldn't help me, nor Ruth, not even your sister, Linda. Although I paid eight hundred dollars for the arrangement for your service, it was pathetic. I'm so sorry. You deserved better. You deserved the best!

I've spent hours looking at the hundreds of photos we took throughout the years. Only now do I realize that while I had eyes to see your beauty, I never really noticed the details. I was a big-picture guy. Looking at your photos has given me a new perspective, a deeper appreciation for how your attention to detail enhanced your natural beauty. Your makeup was always perfect. Who taught you to do that? Not your mother. She didn't wear makeup, just a little powder and lip gloss. Your eyes were stunning, with the longest lashes I've ever seen, and you applied eyeliner, eyeshadow, and mascara with artistic perfection. You were the consummate stylist, coordinating your makeup, your jewelry, your shoes, and your outfit. I wish I had looked at you more closely, the way I now study your photos. Without a doubt, you were the most beautiful woman I've ever seen. Anytime we walked into a room, be it at general council, or the Christian Booksellers Convention, or some other special event, the attendees always turned and looked at us. That doesn't happen anymore. When I enter a room, no one notices. Only now do I realize they weren't looking at us. They were looking at you!

And you were the end-all event planner. Whether I'm remembering Leah's wedding, or a Christmas banquet, or the annual party for the official board, I now realize: You were the best. We never had funds for a professional caterer, so you not only planned the events and decorated the venues, but you also prepared the food. The Christian Chapel board Christmas parties were out of this world. You often spent three full days cooking. I appreciated it then, but only now that you are gone do I understand how rare your gifts and your devotion were. I could go on, but I think you get the point. Without you, I'm just a country bumpkin.

Then there are the book covers. Of course, the publisher has designers who prepare three or four covers for us to choose from, but you always had critical suggestions that enhanced the final product. Were it not for your attention to color and detail, I would have signed off on several covers before they were perfect. I can't help wondering who's going to do that now.

Of course, I wonder about a lot of things now. Who's going to decorate the Christmas tree? Who's going to plan the family birthday parties? Who's going to pick out my shirts? Who's going to cut my hair and trim my beard? Who's going to play backgammon with me? Who's going to critique my sermons? Who's going to take road trips with me? Who's going to encourage me when life gets rough? Who's going to sit on the porch with me and listen to the rain? Who's going to enjoy "our" songs with me? Who's going to sit in the high loft and listen to me read Rod McKuen and James Kavanaugh? Who's going to reminisce with me about our life together? Who's going to . . . The list seems endless.

Although my life is immeasurably diminished without you, in God's eyes I am no less valuable. I am not diminished. I am still called and chosen, still set apart for His service. My life may be diminished without you, but I am not. I am still beloved of the Father. I am still hidden in Christ in God. As Ann Voskamp so eloquently puts it, "I am chosen, accepted, justified, anointed, sealed, forgiven, redeemed, complete, free, Christ's friend, God's child, Spirit's home."[2] Not even your death can change that!

Having said that, let me hasten to add that I have no idea what the rest of my life is going to look like. I'm seventy-six years old. For the last five years, I have been out of active ministry—not by choice but by necessity. Five years ago, you had major brain surgery, followed by a lengthy recovery during which you required my care. Once you recovered, I had three major replacement surgeries (both hips and one knee) in the space of eleven months. Then COVID struck. Following COVID, you were diagnosed with uterine cancer, which required a radical hysterectomy. Now I am grieving your death. At this point, I don't know if there will be any place for me in full-time ministry. Of course, I will continue to write my daily One-Minute Devotions and another book, or maybe three or four more, but beyond that, I have no idea what the future holds. I would like to return to the pulpit, perhaps as a guest speaker or an interim pastor, but that may not happen.

---

[2] Ann Voskamp, "The Broken Way," (Zondervan: Grand Rapids, Michigan 2016), p. 193

Of one thing I am absolutely certain, however. God is with me, and He will direct my steps. When this life is over, when I have finished my course, He will welcome me into His eternal presence. Not only will I rejoice in His presence for all eternity, but I will be reunited with you, the love of my life. And to paraphrase the songwriter, "We will stroll over heaven together some glad day when all our troubles and heartaches are vanished away."

With all my love forever,

Richard

THE ELEVENTH LETTER

*For we know that when this earthly tent we live in is
taken down (that is, when we die and leave this earthly
body), we will have a house in heaven, an eternal body
made for us by God himself and not by human hands.*

2 CORINTHIANS 5:1 NLT

Dearest Brenda:

One year ago, we took a lengthy road trip to see our
dear friends John and Ruth in Naples, Florida. En route, we
visited family and friends. In Gainesville, Florida, we had
dinner with Jim and Dolly. Like you, Dolly was battling
cancer. Unlike you, she chose to take both radiation therapy
and chemotherapy while you chose an alternative treat-
ment. When I saw them a few days ago, her cancer was in

remission, and she was fully recovered from the side effects of her treatments. She was vibrant and full of life.

When I shared that good news with Leah (our daughter), she asked, "How does that make you feel?"

In an instant, I replied, "Thankful."

I'm thankful Dolly is alive and well. I'm thankful Jim can still share life with his wife, and I'm thankful Alexis still has the mother she loves.

And I'm thankful that you are with Jesus, forever free from all pain and suffering. You will never again experience disappointment or sorrow or heartbreak. Am I sad? Of course. Do I miss you? More than anyone will ever know. But I am also thankful!

Then Leah asked a follow-up question. "Do you ever wonder if Mother would still be alive if she had taken radiation and chemo as the oncologist recommended? Do you ever have second thoughts about the choices she made?"

I thought about it for a moment before replying, and then I told Leah that was a decision you made a long time ago. You always said you would never take radiation or chemo. After watching my sister undergo all kinds of treatments, suffer unspeakably, and still die from cancer, you said, "I can't do that." Any number of people may say they won't take chemo or radiation, but when faced with the reality of cancer, they usually change their minds. Your resolve never wavered, not even when it became apparent you were dying.

I'm thankful you had seven months of relatively good health. We got to spend Christmas with Doug and Leah in New York. We took a lengthy road trip to see family and friends. John and Ruth came to see us, as did Lee and Barbara. We visited James River Church in Springfield, Missouri, and took in a show in Branson. Just five weeks before you died, you were swimming in the lake with Kami, Crystal, and their kids. Had you taken chemo and radiation, you couldn't have done all that.

Thinking about it now, I am at peace with your decision. You placed your life in the Lord's hands and trusted Him with the outcome. You believed He had already set a date for your homegoing. Several Scriptures influenced your thinking, probably none more so than Luke 12:25[3] and Psalm 139:16.[4] Nonetheless, not being privy to the day of your departure, we asked the Lord for a miracle. Having witnessed several supernatural healings, we knew God was

---

[3] "And which of you by being anxious can add a single hour to his span of life?" (Luke 12:25 ESV).

[4] "You saw me before I was born. Every day of my life was recorded in your book. Every moment was laid out before a single day had passed" (Psalm 139:16 NLT).

able to heal you, removing every trace of cancer from your body. That was our hope, but like Jesus in Gethsemane, we prayed, "Not our will, but Your will be done" (see Matthew 26:39). If the Lord was not going to heal you supernaturally, we asked Him to take you home quickly and with a minimum of pain, which He did.

Initially I was terribly disappointed that the Lord did not heal you, but as time has passed, *I am coming to realize that what He did is so much better than a physical healing.* Had He healed you, the best we could have hoped for was a few more years of good health, and then you would have had to face suffering and death all over again. From my limited perspective, your death was an unequivocal tragedy, but I was only thinking of my loss, not your gain.

Joe Bayly says, "Death is a wound to the living." Make no mistake, your death wounded me in ways nothing else ever has or ever could, but with each passing day, the Lord is helping me to see things more clearly. Not only are you free from all sickness and disease, but you have also been delivered from all the emotional pain that is so common to our human family. Never again will you spend a sleepless night agonizing over Leah's health or the spiritual condition of your grandchildren. Never again will you suffer regrets over past failures. Never again will you suffer disappointment, or concerns over a world gone mad, or worry over an uncertain future. In the words of the great Negro spiritual, you are, "Free at last! Free at last! Thank God Almighty, you are free at last."

When you passed, only your physical body died. Everything else that made you who you are—your spirit, your soul, your intellect, and your personality—continued to live, but on a far grander scale than anything that exists here on earth. I have no way to conceive of what life is like for you now, for it is completely beyond anything I've ever experienced. Try as I might, I can't wrap my mind around it, nor should I expect to. For "no eye has seen, no ear has heard, and no mind has imagined what God has prepared for those who love him" (1 Corinthians 2:9 NLT). It is enough to know that you are with Christ and more alive than you have ever been before.

I will close with this: Today has been a hard day. I start home in the morning, and I know what awaits me—an empty house full of memories. I want to be home; I just don't want to be home alone. I long for what once was, but I know it can never be again. You are gone, and you are not coming back. Thankfully Jesus is with me. His near presence strengthens me and gives me faith to face an unknown future. My grief, as deep as it is, is richly seasoned with hope. Nothing, not even your passing, can separate me from the love of God that is revealed in Christ Jesus our Lord (see Romans 8:38–39).[5]

With all my love forever,

[signature: Richard]

---

[5] "I am convinced that nothing can ever separate us from God's love. Neither death nor life, neither angels nor demons, neither our fears for today nor our worries about tomorrow—not even the powers of hell can separate us from God's love. No power in the sky above or in the earth below—indeed, nothing in all creation will ever be able to separate us from the love of God that is revealed in Christ Jesus our Lord" (Romans 8:38–39 NLT).

THE TWELFTH LETTER

God is a safe place to hide,
ready to help when we need him.
We stand fearless at the cliff-edge of doom,
courageous in seastorm and earthquake,
Before the rush and roar of oceans,
the tremors that shift mountains.
Jacob-wrestling God fights for us,
God-of-Angel-Armies protects us.

PSALM 46:1–3 MSG

Dearest Brenda:

It's been nearly seven months since you left this world for a better place, and although I am rejoicing for you, I don't think I will ever stop grieving. My grief is not as raw now, and I even have moments when I think I might one day be happy again, or if not happy, at least not so grief-stricken. Yet, I am troubled, too. As my grief wanes, I fear I might forget you, and I never want to do that. Sometimes it feels the only way to hang on to your memory is to hang on to the pain that goes with it. If that's the case, I will gladly take the pain, for I don't want to live a day without your memory. Hopefully that's not the way it's going to be, but who knows?

I have discovered that grief is like the tide. Immediately following your death, the tide of grief came crashing in like a tsunami, threatening to overwhelm me. If it hadn't been for the presence of family and friends, especially John and Ruth, I think it would have crushed me. As the weeks turned into months, I began to notice an emerging pattern. Initially the tide of grief was high and stayed in for a long time. But over time, the high tide receded, at least a little bit, and when it returned, it didn't stay in as long. When the tide goes out, I experience a certain amount of peace. I wouldn't say I am happy, but at least I am not unhappy.

Yesterday I awakened from a deep sleep. The television was on in our bedroom, but the volume was barely audible, the way you used to watch it while I napped. Still only half-awake, I reached across the bed to take your hand, but you weren't there. I couldn't help wondering where you were.

Maybe you were watching television in the living room, or sitting on the glider overlooking the lake, or making dinner in the kitchen. As I came fully awake, I remembered that you were gone, that you had left this world to be with Jesus. In that moment, the grief I experienced was nearly as great as it was when I watched you take your last breath.

Still, as painful as life is without you, I wouldn't bring you back, even if I could. I would never want you to relive the sorrow and disappointment that is so much a part of even the most successful life on this earth. I would never want you to have to endure sickness and death all over again. No matter how much I miss you, I don't want to bring you back! It would be unbelievably selfish to do that.

As I think about it now, I think I have a better understanding of why Jesus wept just before raising Lazarus from the dead. Of course, He was empathizing with Mary, who was grieving her brother's death, but I think it was more than that. Maybe He was weeping because He knew He was about to take Lazarus from Paradise and return him to this world of trouble and sorrow. I can almost imagine Him apologizing to Lazarus: "I'm sorry, dear friend. I know this is not in your best interest—now you will have deal with sickness and death again—but it is for God's glory so that I might be glorified."

If I were able to bring you back, it wouldn't be for God's glory. It would be for me, for my own pleasure. I would treasure every minute spent with you—sitting together on the porch overlooking the lake, holding hands while watching TV, worshiping together at church, taking a road trip to Colorado, going out to dinner and a movie, seeing a show in Branson, visiting with old friends, sitting by the wood-burning stove watching the season's first snow decorate the trees and blanket the ground, spending Christmas with Doug and Leah in upstate New York, or a hundred other ordinary things made special because you were with me. Never again would I take a single minute spent with you for granted.

But that will never be, and since you're not coming back, I will do the next best thing—relive some of the memories we made together. Maybe I can recapture some of the joy of those bygone days. Maybe I can relive some of the excitement we experienced thirty years ago (March 1993), when we drove onto our property on Beaver Lake. There were no improvements—no electrical power, no telephone service, no water, no sewer. It was nine miles to the nearest paved road and twenty-five miles to town. Your mother and dad set up their motor home, and we pitched a tent in preparation for building our first cabin.

We hired a drilling company to drill a water well. Carroll Electric brought power in, and we installed a septic system, but there was no telephone service, none, not even mobile service. For the next six weeks, we worked from can-to-can't roughing in a small cabin. It was spring in the Ozarks, and it was supposed to be warm, but apparently spring didn't get the memo. It might warm up during the day, if it wasn't raining, but overnight the temperatures dropped into the low forties, sometimes even into the thirties. Your parents fared okay in their motor home, but we were freezing in the tent. When we conversed, we could see our breath. Thinking about it now, I can still see you in your sleeping attire—insulated long johns, two pair of wool socks, and a fuzzy winter hat that covered your whole head and tied under your chin. Sexy? Hardly!

Do you remember how crazy things were—and how much we loved it? Late Thursday afternoons, we would rush to Tulsa and get ready for a weekend of ministry. On Friday morning, we would fly out, and I would preach six or seven times before returning home on Monday afternoon. We would race back to our property late that evening and work on our cabin for the next three days and then do it all over again. Everyone who knew you found it hard to believe. Elegant, sophisticated, classy Brenda living in a tent and cooking over a campfire? Never! That's one of the things I loved most about you. You were so adaptable, a woman for all seasons. Nothing ever seemed to phase you.

Disaster struck on the Friday before Mother's Day. Your father was using the chop saw when it collapsed, driving his right hand into the blade, nearly cutting all four of his fingers off. Thankfully Randy was trained in emergency first aid, or your father might have bled out before we got him to the hospital in Rogers, Arkansas. The emergency-room doctors were able to stabilize him, and then he was life-flighted to Tulsa, where surgeons reattached his fingers, but he never regained the full use of his hand.

As traumatic as that was, it did nothing to dampen our enthusiasm, and we returned to work with renewed determination—although now it was just the two of us. You were thrilled when we finally got the cabin closed in so we could abandon the tent and move inside. Of course, it was several more months before we finished installing the plumbing and electrical wiring. Even with running water and electricity, it was pretty primitive, but we loved it. The first two years were nearly idyllic. Without telephone service or television, it was almost like going back in time. On long winter evenings, we read by the wood-burning stove, played table games, or just talked. Sometimes we chose to chat with only a kerosene lamp for light. By the second year, we had telephone service—if you can call a four-party line telephone service. We had a private telephone line and satellite television by the third year, and shortly thereafter, the internet. With all that, we were much better informed, but not nearly as content. Although we lived in the woods, the internet and satellite television brought the world right to our door.

I'm thankful for all the memories, but they do very little to ease the pain of my grief. Now I wander through the cabin, trying to recapture some of the joy that filled it when you were here, but it is no use. The things that once brought me such joy no longer warm my heart. I climb the ladder to the high loft where we spent so many evenings reading *The Alabaster Cross*[6] and *The Letter*,[7] but it's not the same. The chair where you used to sit is empty, and it breaks my heart to know you will never sit in it again.

With an effort, I turn my thoughts to the present. I can't help wondering what the rest of my life is going to look like. I can't imagine leaving Emerald Pointe. I may be alone here, but there is a comfort in familiar things that I cannot imagine in a new place. Will I always live alone? Perhaps, but maybe not. I can't help wondering if I was writing to myself when I penned Diana's final words to Bryan:

---

[6] Richard Exley, *The Alabaster Cross* (Tulsa, OK: Emerald Pointe Books, 2006).

[7] Richard Exley, *The Letter* (Tulsa, OK: Word and Spirit Publishing, 2020).

I want to encourage you to remarry, sooner rather than later. The Bible says it's not good for a man to be alone. That's why God created Eve for Adam, and that's why God created us for each other, but when I am gone, God will have someone else for you. When you find her, you will likely be tempted to feel you cannot love her without betraying your love for me. Nothing could be farther from the truth. You do not have to stop loving me to love her, nor do you have to divide your love between us. A mother does not divide her love between her children; rather, she multiplies it. In the same way, you do not have to love me less to love the woman God has now prepared for you. When I am gone, there will be love enough in your heart for both of us.[8]

Now that I've written that, it sounds like I'm considering remarriage, and I am tempted to delete it, but I don't. Why? Because as crazy as it may be, I have to admit that I have thoughts like that. There's no woman on the horizon, nor am I looking for one. I really don't know how it could ever work. There's not another woman who could compare with you. Besides, I cannot imagine another woman would want to live this far from town. Then there's the cabin. I love the way you decorated it, and I don't want anyone changing a thing. Tell me how that would work. It wouldn't.

---

[8] Ibid., 497.

Well, baby girl, I guess I have rambled enough for now, so I will sign off. Thankfully you are with Jesus, and none of this concerns you. You don't have to worry about me. Jesus is taking care of me, and I'm going to be alright.

With all my love forever,

Richard

THE THIRTEENTH LETTER

For everything there is a season,
a time for every activity under heaven.
A time to be born and a time to die
A time to cry and a time to laugh.
A time to grieve and a time to dance.

ECCLESIASTES 3:1–2, 4 NIV

Dearest Brenda:

You've been gone nearly eight months now, and I still find myself wandering through the house whispering your name and telling you how much I love you. I know you weren't perfect, but for the life of me, I can't seem to remember your idiosyncrasies. Nearly every day I catch myself praying for you. I hear myself asking Jesus to bless you and hold you close to His heart. I know you don't need my prayers. You are with Jesus in that perfect place, where there is no more pain or sorrow. I guess old habits are just hard to break.

Everything reminds me of you—everything! For instance, the soundtrack for *The Man from Snowy River* is playing on the stereo, and I remember how much you liked that movie. When I go to Rogers for groceries, I drive past Shipley Donuts and remember how you always wanted to get a kolache and a bottle of milk, plus a dozen donuts to take home. Or if it is afternoon, I remember how you liked to get a hot-fudge sundae from Andy's Frozen Custard. I haven't gotten donuts or a sundae since you went to be with Jesus. It just wouldn't be the same without you. As far as that goes, nothing is the same without you.

My life may look the same—I still live at Emerald Pointe; I have the same friends, although they don't come around much anymore; I wear the same style of clothes; I drive the same car (in my mind, it will always be *your* car); I attend the same church and do the same things we used to do, but nothing is the same. Nothing!

I continue to make coffee first thing in the morning and unload the dishwasher while it is brewing. Then I do devotions as the sun comes up over the lake. I pray the Lord's Prayer, recite the Ten Commandments, and take communion, just like we did when you were here, but it's not the same. Jesus is just as near and maybe more real to me than

He ever has been, but while He provides comfort, there's still this huge hole in my heart.

Do you remember how Trey would run up to you and say, "I need a hug" when he was just a little guy? Well, I'm not a little guy, but I desperately need a hug. John Merrell put the picture of us kissing as the screensaver on my computer. The photo was taken on your seventy-third birthday, and I look at it every day. What I wouldn't give to hold you in my arms one more time. What I wouldn't give to kiss you once more.

I dream about you virtually every night. The dreams are mostly nonsensical, but they do have a reoccurring theme. I am always searching for you, but I can never find you. In one dream, we were at a large conference where I was scheduled to preach. Somehow we became separated, and I couldn't find you. To make matters worse, I seem to have lost my cell phone, and I can't remember your cell number. Of course, I wake up without finding you, and I am left with an aching emptiness that haunts me for most of the day. Just once I would like to dream something wonderful, like holding hands with you while walking on the beach in Hawaii or holding you in my arms as the moon comes up over Beaver Lake.

Last night I dreamed I wasn't feeling well, so I was wrapped in a blanket sitting on the couch. The details aren't clear, but it seemed a friend or family member was coming to see me. You went into the other room to answer the door or maybe to get something for me. When you didn't return, I went to see what was keeping you, but you were nowhere to be found. I went from room to room calling your name. The last thing I remembered before awakening was frantically calling out, "Brenda Starr, where are you?" I can't help wondering if it will always be this way. Will I spend the rest of my life wandering from place to place, always looking for you, always calling your name?

Now the soundtrack from *Out of Africa* is playing "Let the Rest of the World Go By." At this point in the movie, Robert Redford puts a record on the Victrola and asks Meryl Streep to dance. It is an impossibly romantic scene, and the first time we saw it, you smiled at me and reached for my hand. "Do you want to dance?" you asked in a husky voice, making my heart beat fast. Well, it's playing now, but no one reaches for my hand, no one asks me to dance, and my heart aches.

Why, you may wonder, do I keep doing things that remind me of you if it is so painful? Because as much as it hurts, the memories are all I have left, and I never want to forget you, although I don't think there's any danger of that. We started dating when we were just kids, and for the next sixty-one years, there was never a Richard without a Brenda. And there was never a Brenda without a Richard.

Our lives were so intertwined that I have almost no memories without you.

Now I'm listening to John Denver sing "Back Home Again," and in an instant, I am transported to a Saturday afternoon in 1993. I had been gone for a week leading a marriage retreat for missionaries in Costa Rica, and I can't wait to see you. When I exit the baggage claim area, I see you sitting at the curb in our Nissan Pathfinder. As always you look stunning, and when I get in the car, John Denver is singing "Back Home Again," and I realize you planned it that way. It was your way of saying, "Welcome home, world traveler."

On Easter Sunday, I went to Grace Church in Houston with Tom and Patty. The auditorium is huge, seating nearly ten thousand people, and it was packed. Sitting directly in front of me was a handsome young couple. As the pastor was preaching, the husband reached over and put his hand on his wife's knee. After a moment, she placed her hand on his. It was a tender moment, and in an instant, I forgot the pastor's sermon. All I could think was that I would never again place my hand on your knee. Silent tears escaped my eyes and slid down my cheeks, only to lose themselves in my beard.

Unexpected things like that happen nearly every day, and I wonder if I will ever be able to hear your name without tearing up. I hope not, if that means I've finally gotten over you. I don't want to get over you. As long as I live, I want to hold you in my heart. Someday, however, I do hope I can remember you without grieving, that the memories of the special love we shared will bring me joy and not sorrow.

Well, baby girl, I guess I have run on long enough, so I had better close. Bye for now.

With all my love forever,

[signature: Richard]

THE FOURTEENTH LETTER

One thing I do: Forgetting what is behind and straining
toward what is ahead, I press on toward the goal to win
the prize for which God has called me heavenward in
Christ Jesus.

PHILIPPIANS 3:13–14 NIV

Dearest Brenda:

It is raining today, and it reminds me of the spring thirty years ago when we were building our cabin on Emerald Pointe. We were living in a tent, and it rained nearly every day. Although you sealed and resealed every seam on our tent, we couldn't keep the rain out. Somehow it found every tiny pinhole, and when we awakened each morning, there was a puddle of water in the downhill corners of the tent. You were a trouper. I can't remember you complaining, not once. You simply set to work once more, determined to keep the rain out.

I hated the rain. It made everything we did harder, but today I welcome it. Our cabin is snug and dry, and the sound of the rain on the metal roof sounds like love to me. It reminds me of a rainy afternoon in Holly, Colorado, more than fifty years ago. I was lying on the bed reading a Louis L'Amour western while you napped beside me. Later we made love as the day died outside our window. To this day, it is one of my most treasured memories.

Daily, my memories sing their siren songs, tempting me to live only in the past. They promise a chance to relive special moments from the past, but it's an empty promise. My memories are just that—memories—nothing more. Death has taken you from me, and you are not coming back. As painful as it is, I'm slowly coming to grips with the fact that life can't be lived in the past. At some point, I have to embrace the future, no matter how empty and uncertain it may appear. It's not easy. The past, with its memories, is familiar—it's who I am, who we were, Richard and Brenda—but the future is unknown, and I am alone.

I try to encourage myself by remembering the Lord's faithfulness to us through the years. Early in our ministry, we had some hard times, when our future looked uncertain. In 1972, we suffered several painful rejections, and it seemed there was no place for us in the ministry, but the Lord made a way. Then, from January to June in 1975, we lived in limbo. We had been dismissed from our position as youth pastors, and although we sent out numerous résumés, not a single church responded. In desperation, we cried out to the Lord, promising to go anywhere and do anything, no matter how difficult the task or how small the assignment. A few days later, the Church of the Comforter in Craig, Colorado, called, inviting us to serve as their pastors. Once again, the Lord made a way.

During those difficult days, when it seemed there was no place for us in the ministry, we strengthened one another in the Lord. I am humbled when I remember how you trusted the Lord to guide us. You never seemed to worry. You were so sure He would speak to me. To *me!* Without a moment's hesitation, you followed me wherever the Lord was leading. Not once did you challenge me. If I felt the Lord had spoken, you accepted it. Although that was one of the things I loved most about you, I can't help wondering why you trusted me so completely. I'm grateful you did, but I can't imagine why.

How I wish you were here to encourage me now. It "feels" like I have no ministry, and the enemy tempts me to believe that the ministry the Lord gave me is over. He tells me I have been out of circulation too long, that I'm a forgotten man. He tells me I'm too old, that I don't have anything relevant to share with this generation. I defend myself with the

Word: "Though I walk in the midst of trouble, you preserve my life . . . with your right hand you save me. *The Lord will fulfill his purpose for me* (Psalm 138:7–8 NIV1984, emphasis mine)—but I'm still struggling.

I'm waiting for a word from the Lord, and it's not easy. I sometimes think that "faith to wait" is the most challenging kind of faith. I want to do something—anything. But all I can do right now is wait. I can't decide if the Lord is silent regarding my future or if grief has made me stone-deaf. Either way, I have absolutely no idea what the future holds.

Maybe if I knew what the future was going to look like, I could more readily embrace it. As it is, I feel a little like Abraham must have felt when "he went out, *not knowing where he was going*" (Hebrews 11:8 NKJV, emphasis mine). Not only do I not know where I'm going, but I don't even know how to go out. I am determined to walk through each door the Lord opens, but beyond that, I don't have a clue about my future. Even if ministry as I have known it is over, that doesn't mean my usefulness to the Lord is finished. I'm sure He has a plan, and in His "right" time, He will reveal it.

You have been gone more than eight months now, and I am determined to focus on the future rather than always living in the past, but it's not easy. It feels disloyal, like I'm abandoning you, and I would never do that. Please know that no matter what the future holds, I will always hold you in my heart. Our love will never end. I will always remember your birth date, our wedding anniversary, and of course, the day you went to be with Jesus. Contrary to what many believe, time doesn't heal all wounds. More often than not, it only deepens the wound. At least that's the way it is for me. Every family gathering, every special event, reopens my wound, reminding me that there will always be an empty chair where you should be. Focusing on the future won't change that.

Although it seems my grief is endless, I must be making progress, or how else could I address the future? I will always grieve for you, but I don't want to get trapped in my grief. It will always be a part of my life, but I don't want to allow it to consume me. Although Jesus was a "man of sorrows" and "acquainted with grief" (Isaiah 53:3 NKJV), He was also a gregarious person. Yet beneath His outgoing personality, His heart ached, always ached. That's how I think it will be for me. I will always be grieving for you, even when I am enjoying a meal with friends, or laughing with children, or celebrating at a wedding. Because my love for you will never end, neither will my grief.

With all my love forever,

Richard

THE FIFTEENTH LETTER

The LORD God said, "It is not good for the man to be
alone. I will make a helper suitable for him."
So the LORD God caused the man to fall into a deep
sleep; and while he was sleeping, he took one of the
man's ribs and then closed up the place with flesh. Then
the LORD God made a woman from the rib he had taken
out of the man, and he brought her to the man.
The man said,
"This is now bone of my bones
and flesh of my flesh;
she shall be called 'woman,'
for she was taken out of man."
That is why a man leaves his father and mother and is
united to his wife,
and they become one flesh.

GENESIS 2:18, 21–24 NIV

Dearest Brenda:

When life is grand and things are going well, we naïvely believe it will never end, that life will always go on like this—at least I did. Whether I am talking about our carefree years traveling as young evangelists, or the challenging years serving as pastors of the Church of the Comforter in Craig, Colorado, or the exciting years at Christian Chapel in Tulsa, Oklahoma, I thought they would never end. Oh, I knew we were all getting older and that someday death would claim us, but I felt we were immortal. I should have seen the hand-writing on the wall. Our parents died, as did some dear friends, and then even Sherry, my baby sister. Intellectually I got it, but on an emotional level, it wasn't real. I lived as if it would never happen to us.

Then you had emergency brain surgery. That should have been a wake-up call, but as you recovered, I pushed it to the back of my mind. Four years later, you were diagnosed with uterine cancer, and although we talked about the possibility of your death, I don't think I really believed you were going to die. Even when you spent most of your days lying in bed, you never complained, so it was easy for me to minimize the seriousness of your illness. When I finally had to tell family and friends it didn't look like you had long to live, a part of me still refused to believe you were really dying. And although I prayed for Jesus to make your homegoing peaceful, I still did not fully grasp what was happening.

If I were given a second chance, I would like to think I would never take a single moment for granted. I would like to believe that given another chance, I would live each moment to the very fullest, realizing it might well be our last. After all, what is our life but "a vapor that appears for a little time and then vanishes away" (James 4:14 NKJV)? I think of a hundred special moments, scattered across a lifetime, that I naïvely thought would never end. Things like high school homecoming games, double dates with Foy and Barbara, weekend trips to your grandparents' farm in Cheapside, Thanksgivings at Vallew, listening to your parents tell us about the Great Depression, about life in the 1940s during WWII with its shortages and ration cards. But like a vapor, they just appeared for a moment, then vanished. And now our life together has ended, vanished like the proverbial vapor as well.

I knew my life would be different without you, but I never imagined I would suffer an identity crisis. After all, I am an ordained minister with more than fifty years spent in full-time ministry. I have served as the lead pastor of five churches. I have preached at numerous district events—district councils, district camp meetings, district minister's retreats, district marriage retreats, and district men's events. Ministry has taken me to more than twenty foreign countries and nearly all fifty states. In addition, I have authored forty books and hosted a national radio broadcast, so my identity should be well established.

So, what happened?

You died, and only now do I realize you were the one who validated my identity. When I looked into your eyes, I saw myself. You knew me. You knew my history, you knew who I was, you knew what I had done. Now it feels like no one truly knows me, not the way you did. Without you, I feel unknown, like a nonperson, or at least like a stranger.

I know my identity does not depend on anything I have done, or what anyone thinks of me, but on God and God alone. In the core of my being, I get that, but you were still a huge part of who I was. We had been together since we were just kids, thirteen and fourteen years old. You shared the good times and the hard times; you were part of every significant event in my life and ministry. You stood beside me when we buried my parents and my sister. You celebrated with me when my first book was published, when I received my honorary doctorate, and when I preached at the general council in Argentina. You were part of every significant thing that has ever happened in my life. There was never a Richard without a Brenda. Now there is only a Richard, and without you, I don't know who I am. No wonder God said, "It is not good for the man to be alone" (Genesis 2:18 NKJV). I am alone, and it isn't good; in fact, it's nearly killing me.

Years ago, we taught a marriage class using Walter Wangerin Jr.'s book *As for Me and My House.* In my youthful naïveté, I thought I understood what he was saying when he wrote, "Personal meaning and human value arise only in relationship. Solitude casts doubt on them. Identity, too, is discovered only in relationship. . . . It always takes another person to show myself to me. Alone, I die."[9]

Only now, since death has taken you from me, am I beginning to understand. It always takes another person to show myself to me. Not just any person, but that one special person whom God joined together with me till death do us part. As Wangerin puts it, "It is more than comfort we receive from other people: it is identity, so I know who I am. It is being itself, and the conviction of personal worth."[10]

My résumé looks the same, but without you it seems empty somehow. I don't mean to belittle all the Lord has allowed me to do. I'm truly grateful, but without you, I don't have anyone to share it with. My greatest joy was sharing life with you. How many times did I lie beside you at night, holding your hand, and tell you, "I would rather be here with you than any place in the world"? More times than I can count! You completed me, made me who I am, and now I feel lost without you.

---

[9] Walter Wangerin Jr., *As for Me and My House* (Nashville, TN: Thomas Nelson, 1987), p. 58.

[10] Ibid., p. 58.

I try to comfort myself with the thought of spending eternity with you, but I can't help wondering if we will have the same special relationship in heaven. Will you still be that one person who validates me, who shows myself to me, who lets me know who I am? I don't think so, for Jesus said, "After the dead are raised up, we're past the marriage business. As it is with angels now, *all our ecstasies and intimacies then will be with God*" (Mark 12:25 MSG, emphasis mine). If that's the way it is going to be, I know that will be all I need, but right now, the thought of it makes me sad. I take comfort by reminding myself that everything in heaven is far better than anything here on earth. That being the case, how can we doubt that our most intimate earthly relationships will not be enhanced in heaven? I hope C.S. Lewis was correct when he wrote, "I think the union between the risen spouses will be as close as that between the soul and its own risen body."[11] May it be so, Lord Jesus.

With all my love forever,

[signature: Richard]

---

[11] C.S. Lewis, quoted in Sheldon Vanauken. *A SevereMercy* (New York: Harper & Row, 1977), 205.

THE SIXTEENTH LETTER

There is laid up for me the crown of righteousness,
which the Lord, the righteous Judge, will give to me on
that Day, and not to me only but also to all who have
loved His appearing.

2 TIMOTHY 4:8 NKJV

Dearest Brenda:

Although you have been gone nearly ten months now, this week has been one of the hardest. In some ways, grief seems to be doing its healing work, but in other ways, my grief feels as raw as it was immediately after your death. It only takes a poignant memory, a few words from a familiar song, or the mention of your name to cause my throat to constrict and my eyes to tear up. There's been a lot of that this week as I approached what would have been our fifty-seventh wedding anniversary. For more than fifty years, June 10th was our special day. Now it's just a painful reminder that you are gone, and you are not coming back.

Fifty-seven years ago today, I drove to the historic Warwick Hotel overlooking Herman Park in Houston, Texas. I was only nineteen years old, and its opulent splendor intimidated me. For just a moment, I considered driving away and finding a more modest hotel or even a motel for our wedding night. Resisting that impulse, I squared my shoulders and marched up to the front desk. After checking in, I followed the bellman to our room, where he deposited our luggage. When he left, I looked around the room, thinking that in just a few hours you and I would be sharing our first night together.

Our wedding was all I hoped it would be. You were dazzling in your wedding gown as your father walked you down the aisle. My knees were shaking as I took your hand and turned to face our pastor, the Reverend W.A. Majors. After we said our vows, we knelt and sang "I'll Go Where You Want Me to Go." We wanted our first act as a married couple to be a declaration of our commitment to the Lord. It was a commitment you lived out all the days of your life. Never once did you hesitate to go where the Lord was calling us. What an asset you were to the ministry and to me.

By today's standards, the reception in the church's fellowship hall was modest—just cake and punch—but in my mind, it seemed to go on forever. Finally, you changed into your going-away suit of pink lace, and we ran toward our 1966 Mustang under a deluge of rice thrown by our family and friends. Although I was eager to go to the hotel, we enjoyed a leisurely dinner at an expensive restaurant before finally driving to the hotel.

There was no exotic honeymoon for us, just one night in the historic Warwick Hotel before we moved into our tiny one-bedroom apartment. We were so much in love and so happy we couldn't wait to share our joy with our families. When we left the hotel, we drove directly to your parents' home. A couple days later, you fixed dinner for my parents in our small apartment. Sharing our joy with those we loved made it even better. Your favorite memory was going to the Ringling Bros. Barnum & Bailey Circus in the Astrodome. My favorite was just being with you.

In the ensuing years, we celebrated fifty-six anniversaries, and most of them are engraved on my memory. Foy and Barbara Clark, our dearest friends, celebrated our first anniversary with us at Jimmy Walker's Seafood Restaurant in Kemah, Texas. We celebrated our third anniversary at a rustic steakhouse in Lamar, Colorado. Bob and Diane Arnold gave us a Polaroid camera as an anniversary present that year, and I took pictures of you in the lingerie I bought you. There was not much of a celebration on our fourth anniversary, as you were recovering from emergency surgery following Leah's birth.

We celebrated our tenth anniversary in a condo on the ski slopes in Steamboat Springs, Colorado. Following Leah's wedding in 1988, we rented a rustic cabin above Meeker, Colorado, and spent a week alone in the Rockies, celebrating twenty-two years of marriage. The accommodations left a lot to be desired, but we enjoyed horseback rides, the fresh mountain air, the solitude, and reading together by kerosene lamplight at night. One of your favorite anniversaries was the one we celebrated with our special friends Keith and Megan Provance, whose anniversary was also on June 10th. Keith arranged for a limousine to pick us up and take us to the Atlantic Sea Grill, where you enjoyed your favorite food—Alaskan king crab. Of course, there was our twenty-fifth anniversary, which was hosted by Christian Chapel. We spent a week on Beaver Lake in Northwest Arkansas and fell in love with it. We ended up buying six acres of land with nearly a thousand feet of lakefront as an anniversary present to ourselves. Two years later, we built a small cabin overlooking Beaver Lake, which we eventually enlarged into a full-sized house.

As I relive all our special anniversaries, I am overwhelmed with emotion. Of course, there is joy, but there is also grief. If I were to tell you the absolute truth, I would have to admit that at the moment, my grief outweighs whatever joy the memories bring. That being the case, you may wonder why I do this to myself. I will tell you why. As painful as the memories are, they are all I have left of us. I embrace them because I never want to forget you. In time, I believe my grief will diminish—not go away, but fade, to be replaced by the joy of the love we shared. But for now, I will embrace it.

If you were here with me, I would make our fifty-seventh anniversary the best one ever. We would do whatever you wanted to do. If you wanted to go to Colorado, we would go to all your favorite places. From Twin Lakes, we would drive over Independence Pass into Aspen. Or we could go over Trail Ridge Pass into Estes Park. We could go to Black Mountain, where we took so many outdoor portraits, or visit Fish Creek Falls near Steamboat Springs. One of my biggest regrets is that I didn't get to take you back to Colorado. You talked about it often, but cancer cut your life short, and now it is too late.

Or, if you didn't feel up to a trip to Colorado, we could take a drive through the Ozarks and visit some of the places you were always showing me in the *Arkansas Living* magazine. Or maybe we could go to Branson and take in a show. You always loved doing that. I would love to take you to Ruth's Chris Steak House one more time. I would ask the chef to prepare his best meal for us—maybe crabcakes for appetizers, bone-in filet mignon as an entrée and crème brûlée for dessert. I would spare no expense! Only the best for you.

If you didn't feel well enough for any of that, we could just sit in the glider overlooking the lake as the moon came up. We could reminisce about our life together, laughing over the crazy times, crying over the mistakes we made, but mostly just thanking the Lord for His goodness toward us. If I had it to do all over again, I would choose you. I would choose to love and cherish you all the days of my life.

I don't have many regrets, but I must tell you that I wish I had lived a little more extravagantly. If anyone ever deserved the finer things of life, you did. You were a classy lady who had to live most of your life on a pastor's salary. How I wish I could have given you more. My only consolation is that now you have the very best! Never again will you have to make do. Never again will you have to buy your clothes at a consignment store or bring a flawed garment home and remake it. You always looked stunning, and you did it on a budget—but never again. Now you have a crown of life, which the Righteous Judge gave you, and you are decked out in heavenly splendor.

While you are celebrating in heaven, I am grieving deeply, but even in my grief, I choose to be thankful. I am thankful we were allowed to spend our entire married life in the ministry. I am thankful the Lord blessed us with a wonderful daughter and two incredible grandchildren. I am thankful that Alexandria is happily married, and that Deuce is preparing for the ministry. I am thankful for an extended family who loves and supports me during this difficult time. And I thank the Lord for a host of friends who support me with their presence and their prayers. Most of all, I am thankful for the Lord's nearness and for the promise of eternal life. One day soon, I will see you again! Oh, happy day!

With all my love forever,

Richard

THE SEVENTEENTH LETTER

*For I know that my Redeemer lives. . . . And after my
skin is destroyed, this I know, that in my flesh I shall
see God, whom I shall see for myself, and my eyes shall
behold, and not another.*

JOB 19:25–27 NKJV

Dearest Brenda:

One year ago today, an ambulance transported you to
the Circle of Life hospice facility in Bentonville, Arkansas.
At the time, we thought you were simply going in to have
your abdomen drained. Little did we know that four days
later, you would depart this world to be with Jesus. Nothing
in my life has ever impacted me the way your death did. I
had trouble sleeping, my digestive system gave me fits, and
the stress pinched a nerve in my neck, causing severe pain in

my left arm and hand, making it impossible for me to use that arm. As difficult as those physical problems were, they were nothing compared to the pain in my heart. Losing you literally shattered my heart.

My grief was not only physical, but emotional and spiritual as well. Emotionally it seemed all the color had been sucked out of my life. It felt like I was living in a nuclear wasteland, everything was gray and barren. The things that once brought me joy—reading a good book, listening to a favorite song, conversation with a dear friend—now held no interest for me. It was like I was sleepwalking, just going through the motions, not really living.

Spiritually I had moments when I sensed the Lord's presence, but for the most part, I was functioning on autopilot. I maintained the disciplines of a lifetime, by rote mostly—Bible reading, prayer, holy communion, and public worship—but it didn't feel real. To make matters worse, the enemy wrought havoc in my mind, tormenting me with memories of every painful moment in our marriage, tempting me to question all the wonderful times we shared. Were those special times real or just a façade? He even tempted me to question whether you truly loved me. As long as you were alive, I never questioned your love, but once you died, I was haunted by doubts.

Thankfully I was surrounded by family and friends who refused to allow me to wallow in my grief. They were more than willing to walk through the valley of the shadow of death with me, but they refused to let me stay there. Instead, they encouraged me with their memories. I drew strength from them as they reminisced about the life you and I shared. They helped me remember what a special love we had. We were childhood sweethearts. I was only nineteen years old when we married, and you were one year younger. For fifty-six years, two months, and fifteen days, we lived life together, weathering whatever storms and hardships life threw at us, but never once giving up on our marriage. How dare I let the enemy tempt me to doubt your love now that you are gone.

Spiritually he tempted me to doubt the reality of eternal life. Even now he tries to convince me that when you died, you ceased to exist. When he does, I defend myself with the Word: "Jesus said unto her, 'I am the resurrection, and the life: he that believeth in me, though he were dead, yet shall he live'" (John 11:25).

You believed in Jesus, and although your body perished, you are still alive. Everything that made you Brenda Starr has continued to live after you departed this life. In fact, you are more alive right now than you ever were while here on earth. One day soon, I, too, will shed this mortal body, but everything that makes me who I am will continue to live. In eternity, we will be reunited with each other and our loved ones. Here's how the Bible describes it: "He breathed his last and died, and was *gathered to his people*" (Genesis 25:17 NKJV, emphasis mine).

I love that. When we die, we are "gathered to our people," that is, to our family and friends who have gone before us.

While that knowledge comforts me, I still grieve. There will always be a broken place inside me, a place only you can fill. The road you walked wasn't without its share of disappointments, and you suffered some wounds along the way. Everyone does. None of us lives a sinless life, and although the Lord does not treat us as our sins deserve or reward us according to our iniquities (see Psalm 103:10–12), we are often tormented by the memory of past failures and the unintended consequences they wrought.

Like all of us, you lived with regrets. I knew you did, but you were such a private person, I had no idea how you suffered until after you passed. The depth of your pain was revealed when Leah asked for your Bible. I located it, and when I opened it, I discovered you had written a note on the flyleaf: *Upon my death, I would like my Bible presented to my daughter, Leah Starr Exley Baker, as a token of my undying love for her precious life, which was given to me on May 27, 1970.* Then you penned these words to her: *You were the prettiest little thing I'd ever seen, and you became my whole life. The joy you brought to our family and to my life was immeasurable and incomprehensible. I will always treasure the opportunity God gave me to be your mother.*

Next, I opened your Bible to the place you had marked with the ribbon bookmark: 2 Samuel 18. You had underlined verse 33: "O my son Absalom! My son, my son Absalom! If only I had died instead of you" (NIV). In the margin, you wrote: *Leah, if only I could be sick instead of you. Please forgive me. I'm so sorry. I love you so.* I wept when I read your words. My heart hurt when I realized afresh how you grieved over the things Leah suffered.

As I write these words, Casting Crowns is singing "Scars in Heaven." Their lyrics remind me that you are with Jesus in a place where there is no more sorrow or suffering, no more shame or regret. Never again will you be tormented by the memory of past failures. "The thought that makes me smile now, even as the tears fall down, is that the only scars in Heaven are on the hands that hold you now."[12]

With all my love forever,

Richard

---

[12] "Scars in Heaven," by Casting Crowns, was written by Mark Hall and Matthew West. Casting Crowns released "Scars in Heaven" on June 4, 2021.

THE EIGHTEENTH LETTER

Weeping may remain for a night,
but rejoicing comes in the morning. . . .
You turned my wailing into dancing;
You removed my sackcloth
and clothed me with joy. . . .
O LORD my God,
I will give you thanks forever.

PSALM 30:5, 11–12 NIV1984

Dearest Brenda:

Just over one year ago, you left this world for a better place—a place where there is no more sickness or death, no more sorrow or pain. Your suffering was finally over. Never again would you experience pain or sorrow, but my suffering was just beginning. In the ensuing weeks and months,

I would endure unspeakable grief as I tried to learn to live without you. Well do I remember thinking, *So this is what my life is going to be like.* Never had I felt so totally alone.

Thankfully family and friends rallied around me. John and Ruth Merrell arrived from Florida a few hours after you died and stayed for the better part of three weeks. John helped me with the details of your memorial service while Ruth boxed up your clothes for John and me to take to Goodwill. When they departed to return home, I wandered through the house. The evidence of your presence was everywhere, but you were gone, and you weren't coming back. Never had the house seemed so desolate, so empty.

I read and reread parts of *The Letter,* marveling again how, in retrospect, it seemed I was writing our story. Bryan grieved unspeakably as he watched Diana fight a losing battle with breast cancer. When I wrote it, I had no idea that malignant cells had invaded your body and were already doing their evil work. Nor did I have any idea what the future had in store for us—numerous visits to doctors, gynecologists, surgeons, oncologists, and finally hospice care. When it became apparent that you did not have long to live, we had the kind of "hard" conversations I wrote about in *The Letter*:

> *My chest is tight, and it feels like I've been holding my breath forever. When I try to speak, my words come out*

in a croak, and then I am sobbing. After I finally manage to get my emotions under control, I say, "Wow . . . This isn't how I expected our evening to go. I thought we would drink hot chocolate while soaking in the hot springs, maybe smooch a little, and reminisce about the good times we've had."

She squeezes my hand, and for a time, neither of us speaks. Then she says, "There's just one more thing."

"Okay," I say, as I brace myself.

"Bryan, you're still a young man, and I don't want you to spend the rest of your life alone."

I start to protest, but she places her finger on my lips to silence me. She is trembling, and I can only imagine the toll this conversation has taken on her.

"I know how much you love me, and I'm sure you can't conceive of ever getting married again, but in time that will change. Your heart will heal, and when it does, I want you to know you have my blessing to fall in love again. Just promise that you'll never forget me."

She's weeping now, and I hold her close, my tears mingling with hers. When I am finally able to speak, I say, "I could never forget you. Never."[13]

---

[13] Richard Exley, *The Letter* (Tulsa, OK: Word and Spirit Publishers, 2021), pp. 474-475.

When we had our "hard" conversations, I couldn't imagine ever falling in love with anyone else. We were just kids when we fell in love, and I've loved you my whole life. I never dated another girl. As the weeks turned into months following your death, I thought about you constantly. I played and replayed the memories of our life together, and each time I did, it seemed I fell in love with you all over again. I hated living alone, but it was you I wanted and only you. I couldn't imagine loving anyone else.

But God had other plans, and I awoke early on a Tuesday morning a couple days after Easter. As always, my first thought was of you, and I breathed a prayer asking the Lord to help me make it through another day without you. Downstairs Don and Melba were still sleeping, or at least they hadn't yet emerged from their bedroom, so I decided not to get up just yet. As I drifted in and out of sleep, I suddenly thought of Karen West. I have no idea where that thought came from, God maybe, but I couldn't get it out of my mind. On an impulse, I decided to see if she was on Facebook. She was, so I sent her a private message asking if I could call her sometime.

She replied almost immediately saying she would enjoy hearing from me. According to her information on Facebook, she was serving as the senior adult pastor at Cornerstone Community Church in the Fort Worth area. Since I was just a few miles away, in nearby Midlothian, I decided to invite her to lunch. I was driving home later that day, and I had no idea when I might be in the area again.

We met at Olive Garden. To my way of thinking, it wasn't a date. It was just two old friends getting together for lunch. Even though I refused to think of it as a "date," I still felt awkward. Although you had been gone for nearly eight months, in my mind I was still married. It felt strange to be having lunch with another woman, but I soon grew comfortable. In fact, Karen and I talked for nearly two hours, catching up on our families and friends. Since both of us had spent our entire adult lives in ministry, we had much in common, including a host of friends. Karen reminded me that you were her first friend when she and Jimmy moved to Houston and started attending Manor Assembly of God. As we talked, I remembered that she had played the organ and sang in our wedding.

Over the next several weeks, I began calling her, at first every two or three days and then every day. As we talked, I discovered I no longer felt totally alone. I still missed you and grieved every day, but I was starting to feel happy too. When I felt myself developing feelings for Karen, I decided to call Leah. If Leah was opposed to my relationship with Karen, then any thought of marriage had to be put on hold. No way was I going to do anything to add to her grief. Much to my surprise, she encouraged me. "Dad," she said, "this is the first time I have heard a smile in your voice since Mother died. If Karen can make you smile again, I'm all for it."

I was hesitant to tell my family and friends about my relationship with Karen. It had nothing to do with her. I was proud of her. She was an ordained Assemblies of God minister who had served as a pastor's wife, an evangelist, and a missionary. She loved Jesus passionately and served Him with a devotion that inspired everyone who knew her. She was a gifted teacher and musician. She was faith-filled, she was an encourager, and people loved her. So, what was my problem? I was afraid my family and friends would think I was being disloyal to you if I gave my heart to Karen.

It turns out I had no reason to be concerned. When I told them I had asked Karen to marry me, they were thrilled for me. My cell phone exploded with text messages wishing us God's best for our new life together. Karen's friends responded the same way. Here's a sample of the messages we received. This one was written by your dearest friend, Ruth Merrell.

Reading in one of my favorites this morning—Psalms. And I immediately thought of you . . . and Karen. The miracle of your love. So, I am sharing my praise to our amazing God.

Wow! When I think about how earnestly John and I sought divine solace and guidance for you—and how generously He answered—I stand amazed!!!

Psalm 37:23–24 (NLT) says, "The LORD directs the steps of the godly. He delights in every detail of their lives. Though they stumble, they will never fall, for the LORD holds them by the hand."

Thank You, thank You, Jesus, for daily, in the midst of uncertainty and grief, directing Richard's every step. Providing strength, wisdom, courage for every day when his own strength was failing. You have truly been his daily bread, his daily provision! The ungodly world says, "The devil is in the details"—but not so! As Your child, a member of Your eternal Kingdom, Your Word says that it is YOU who are in the details! YOU, my Father, know each step, each mile, each burden, each relationship, each breath of Your children. YOU know every location, timing, and detail of Your inexhaustible provision! Oh, Your amazing love for Your children whom You surround even in the midst of sorrows. Oh, the goodness of being held in Your hand when our feet would stumble, our lives would be diminished and full of grief. Oh, the generosity of Your heart for Richard, to have a helper, a soul mate, a lover—tucked away in Your eternal plan. Thank You, Lord, for being "God of the Details"! The good, good

Father who DELIGHTS in working all things together for good. To You be the glory, honor, and praise for ever and ever!!

Amen

P.S. John and I are thrilled for you and your bride-to-be!!! And we will be there to celebrate with you!

Originally, we had planned to have a small wedding just for our immediate families, but as the news spread, more and more people contacted us to say they wanted to attend, never mind that several of them would have to drive hundreds of miles. We now have more than 150 confirmed guests. My brother Don will perform the ceremony. Deuce (my grandson) will be my best man. Alexia (my granddaughter) will be a bridesmaid, and Renay (Karen's daughter) will be her maid of honor and will also bless our marriage. Leah will sing.

In four days, I will watch Karen walk down the aisle to join me at the altar. There, we will pledge our vows to God and to each other, and there we will be joined together as husband and wife. As I think about it now, I find myself returning once again to something I wrote in *The Letter*. Just before she died, Diana penned a letter to be mailed to Bryan one year after her death. In it, she wrote:

My Dearest Bryan:

If you are reading this letter the first anniversary of my death has passed. I cannot even imagine how difficult the last year has been for you. I trust that the God of all comfort has been very near to you, and I pray that your grief has been richly seasoned with hope—the hope of eternal life!

No husband could ever love a wife more than you have loved me. You have made these difficult days not only bearable, but also blessed. Truly my heart will always be yours.

Now comes the most difficult part of this letter for me. I want to encourage you to remarry, sooner rather than later. The Bible says it's not good for a man to be alone. That's why God created Eve for Adam, and that's why God created us for each other, but when I am gone, God will have someone else for you. When you find her, you will likely be tempted to feel you cannot love her without betraying your love for me. Nothing could be farther from the truth. You do not have to stop loving me to love her, nor do you have to divide your love between us. A mother does not divide her love between her children; rather, she multiplies it. In the same way, you do not have to love me less in order to love the woman God has now prepared for you. When I am gone, there will be love enough in your heart for both of us.[14]

I think the Lord helped me write that to prepare me for this moment. Although I love Karen as much as I am capable of loving anyone, I do not love you any less than I always have. *Truly, now that you are gone, there is love enough in my heart for both of you.* I have loved you nearly all my life, and I always will, but as Ecclesiastes says, there is "a time to weep and a time to laugh, a time to mourn and a time to dance" (3:4 NIV). My time of grieving is drawing to a close. Even as I give thanks for the wonderful life we shared, it is now time for me to begin a new chapter in my life. Thank you, Brenda, for the memories and for loving me.

With all my love forever,

[signature]

---

[14] Ibid., pp. 496-497.

ACKNOWLEDGMENTS

As a minister for nearly sixty years and the author of two previous books on grief, I thought I knew what to expect when a loved one died. Yet nothing prepared me for the storm of emotions that swept over me when Brenda, the love of my life and my wife for fifty-six years, passed. Had it not been for the presence and the prayers of my family and friends, I don't know how I would have made it. They were my lifeline.

Thank you, Leah Starr Baker, for your daily phone calls and encouraging words. Your tribute to Brenda and your song at her service was a gift I will always treasure.

Thank you, Don and Melba Exley, for your prayers. Don, your sermon at Brenda's memorial service was perfect.

Thank you, Alexia Giallonardo, for your wise words of comfort.

Thank you, Deuce Baker, for praying with me in the chapel.

Thank you, Tommy and Shirley King, for never leaving my side as Brenda went to be with Jesus.

Thank you, John and Ruth Merrell, for helping me through the dark days immediately following Brenda's death. Ruth, your eulogy for Brenda was one for the ages!

Thank you, Travis and Kami Elam, for opening your home and your hearts to me. Thanks for making me a part of your family and for nursing me back to health.

Thank you, Keith and Carol Butler, for being my pastors and my friends. You are the best.

Thank you, Rev. Ronnie Morris, for presenting the Christian flag to me at Brenda's memorial service. I will cherish it.

Thank you to Lee and Barbara Clark, Rev. Frank and Linda Cargill, Grant and Susan Cherry, and Charles and Vergie Walker, for being there for Brenda and me.

Thank you to all my family and friends who dropped everything to journey to Arkansas to stand beside me as we bid Brenda goodbye. At the risk of forgetting someone, I want to mention you by name: Douglas Baker, Brandon Giallonardo, Linda Thompson, Scott and Melanie Miller, Bob and Anita Exley, Bobby Exley Jr., Dan and Heather Feimster, Ali Jacobson, Jason and Renee Exley, Eric and Crystal McCarty, Dustin and Sabrina Hackney, Tom and Patty Echols, Keith and Megan Provance, Jake and Leah Provance, Denny and Sandy Miller, Bob and Sherilyn Cook, Gary and Wilma Davidson, Douglas Fullenwider, Bo Melin, Greg and Marilynda Lynch, Carol Holderness, Jerry and Barbra Russell, George and Linda Wiland, Billy Wiland, Jody Streck, Barry and Margo Tims, Bill and Trudy Tims, Diane Hill, and all my Christian Chapel friends.

When I think of each of you, I am reminded of the apostle's words in 2 Corinthians 7:6 (NIV): *"But God, who comforts the downcast, comforted us by the coming of Titus."* Even as the Lord used Titus to comfort Paul and his missionary team, so He used each one of you to comfort me.

ABOUT THE AUTHOR

Richard Exley enjoys quiet talks with old friends, kerosene lamps, good books, a warm fire when the weather turns cold and a good cup of coffee any time. He has been a pastor, conference and retreat speaker, as well as a radio broadcaster. In addition he has written more than 35 books including *Authentic Living, The Rhythm of Life, The Making of a Man, Man of Valor, When You Lose Someone You Love, Dancing in the Dark, The Alabaster Cross* and *The Letter. The Making of a Man* was one of five finalists for the Gold Medallion Devotional Book of the Year. In 2003 the Methodist Episcopal Church USA and the National Clergy Council Board of Scholars awarded him the Doctorate of Divinity honoris causa for his life's work in ministry and writing. Whether we are talking about his novels or his books on marriage, men, or ministry his spiritual insights always provide encouragement. His greatest strength however is comforting those who grieve.

Please visit the author and check out his podcasts at

RichardExleyMinistriesandBooks.com.

You may contact the author at

pastorrichardexley@gmail.com.

OTHER BOOKS BY RICHARD EXLEY

When You Lose Someone You Love

From Grief to Gratefulness

Storm Shelter

Hearing God

The Alabaster Cross (a novel)

The Letter (a novel)

The Making of a Man

Man of Valor

Encounters at the Cross

Encounter with Christ

Intimate Moments for Couples

Perils of Power

The Gift of Gratitude

The One-Minute Devotion

Authentic Living

The Rhythm of Life

Blue Collar Christianity

www.RichardExleyBooks.com